SOCIAL THEORY: A BIBLIOGRAPHIC SERIES

No. 27

MICHEL FOUCAULT (II): A BIBLIOGRAPHY

compiled by Joan Nordquist

Reference and Research Services

<u>MICHEL FOUCAULT (II): A BIBLIOGRAPHY</u>

ISBN 0-937855-53-7
Social Theory: A Bibliographic Series, No. 27
ISSN 0887-3577

Published in 1992 by
Reference and Research Services
511 Lincoln Street
Santa Cruz, CA 95060 USA

Social Theory: A Bibliographic Series will issue four bibliographies a year. Subscriptions are $45/year; $15 each individual bibliography

"Michel Foucault: An Introduction" by Katherine Davis included with the permission of the author.

TABLE OF CONTENTS

Introduction to SOCIAL THEORY: A BIBLIOGRAPHIC SERIES

There is intense interest among users of large libraries in publications by and about a number of social theorists, such as Jurgen Habermas, Jacques Derrida, Michel Foucault, Herbert Marcuse and others. There are frequently articles about, or references to, these thinkers in a wide range of the more important newspapers, cultural periodicals and in scholarly journals. Also, they are often referred to in college and university lectures and cited in introductory texts and readers in all the social sciences and most of the humanities -- in philosophy as well as anthropology, in literature as well as sociology, in theology and law as well as political science. To paraphrase Clifford Geertz, they are cited everywhere, by everybody, for all sorts of purposes. In a world beset by social and economic problems, the theoretical perspective is "in" in the search for understanding and solutions by the general intellectual community, and there are many indications that this perspective is growing.

It is a pleasure, therefore, to welcome the appearance of a new bibliographic series which will provide quick and easy reference both to these social theorists and to many of the problems they and others commonly focus on.

In the case of the theorists, there are two bibliographic problems. First, they are quite prolific and their publications are widely reprinted in whole or in part, and extracts which are reprinted may be given new titles. Secondly, the number of people who may look for a particular publication by one of them is quite large. There is, consequently, a need both for comprehensive bibliographies on these individuals and a need for quick and easy reference to their major publications and to where these may be found in the original, in translation and in their various reprinted forms. One of the great virtues of a quick and easy reference work on Michel Foucault, for example, will show that his essay "What is an author?" can be found in his book Language, Counter-Memory, Practice and also in Textual Strategies: Perspectives in Post-Structuralist Criticism, edited by Josue V. Harari. If one title is not available in a library, either because it is not owned or because it is checked out, perhaps the other will be. A quick and easy bibliography is a most useful guide to the literature, for those interested in theory and its applications are just as interested in finding a publication right now as any other users of libraries. The recent comprehensive bibliography on Foucault does not meet this standard of being quick and easy to use. The series, **Social Theory: A Bibliographic Series**, does meet that standard and need.

The series, **Social Theory: A Bibliographic Series**, should be in all college and university libraries and in all public libraries servicing a general intellectual community. They will be used often by librarians and by the users of those libraries.

Rex Beckham
Reference Librarian
University of California, Santa Cruz

Introduction to Bibliography No. 27

MICHEL FOUCAULT (II)

The primary purpose of the bibliography is to provide access to the essays and books of Michel Foucault in the English language. Critical literature about the work of the theorist is also presented. All materials in English in the bibliographic sources examined are included. The bibliographic sources consulted are listed on page 8. The bibliography supplements the bibliography MICHEL FOUCAULT (Social Theory: A Bibliographic Series, No. 4) published in 1986. All the books and essays by Foucault reprinted since 1985 have been added to Sections I and II in this new edition. All the critical literature about Foucault published since 1985 has been added to Sections I and III. Section IV contains works about Foucault published since 1985.

Section I. contains the books written by Michel Foucault in English. Also included are his books written originally in French. Listed under each book title are book reviews and essays about that particular book. All essays and reviews are placed under the English edition. Book notes and short reviews (100-300 words) are not included.

Essays, interviews and excerpts from books by Foucault are listed in **Section II.** The works are arranged alphabetically by title followed by the sources of reprints arranged chronologically. An **KEY-WORD-IN-TITLE INDEX** can be found on page 39.

Section III. lists books in English about the work of Michel Foucault. Bibliographies are cited on page 46.

Section IV. contains the critical literature in English about Foucault. These articles are drawn from two sources: (1) articles in books and (2) journal articles. This section includes all materials found in the bibliographic sources checked for the period 1985 to 1992. Bibliographies in periodicals and in books are listed on page 68. A **KEYWORD-IN-TITLE INDEX** is provided on page 69.

KEYWORD-IN-TITLE INDEXES are provided for the essay material in Sections II and IV. Because the keywords are not always significant, "Title Enrichment Terms", in the manner used by ART AND HUMANITIES CITATION INDEX, are added when necessary to enhance the indexes.

BIBLIOGRAPHIC SOURCES

BIBLIOGRAPHIC INDEX
PHILOSOPHERS INDEX
SOCIOLOGICAL ABSTRACTS
PSYCHOLOGICAL ABSTRACTS
SOCIAL SCIENCES INDEX
HUMANITIES INDEX
SOCIAL SCIENCES CITATION INDEX
ART AND HUMANITIES CITATION INDEX
MLA BIBLIOGRAPHY
LITERARY CRITICISM REGISTER
BRITISH HUMANITIES INDEX
ESSAY AND GENERAL LITERATURE
ALTERNATIVE PRESS INDEX
THE LEFT INDEX
FRENCH XX BIBLIOGRAPHY
ART INDEX
ART BIBLIOGRAPHIES MODERN
RILM: INTERNATIONAL REPERTORY OF THE LITERATURE OF ART
BHA: BIBLIOGRAPHY OF THE HISTORY OF ART
INTERNATIONAL INDEX TO FILM PERIODICALS
FILM LITERATURE INDEX
BOOK REVIEW INDEX
BOOK REVIEW DIGEST
AN INDEX TO BOOK REVIEWS IN THE HUMANITIES
COMBINED RETROSPECTIVE INDEX TO BOOK REVIEWS IN SCHOLARLY JOURNALS
NATIONAL UNION CATALOG
BOOKS IN PRINT
FORTHCOMING BOOKS IN PRINT
INTERNATIONAL BOOKS IN PRINT
WHITAKER'S BOOKS IN PRINT
CURRENT CONTENTS (on-line)
MAGAZINE INDEX (on-line)
MEDLINE (on-line)

Books on the topics of poststructuralism, aesthetics, philosophy, literary theory, social theory and French intellectual history were examined for articles and bibliographies.

Michel Foucault (1926-1984), French philosopher and historian, explored themes including psychiatry, medicine, linguistics, modern penal practice, and sexuality, and their historical antecedents in order to articulate systems of thought and their evolution. He sought to illustrate the relationship between "knowledge," and the social practices and power relations through which it is developed and applied. Influenced by structuralism, he stressed the importance of what is and can be said and the belief that discourse is an unconscious reflection of entrenched presuppositions.

Foucault didn't regard history as a total process with an intelligible meaning; rather, it is marked by radical discontinuities. Concepts by which we define ourselves appear and disappear abruptly. "Normality," "sexuality," or even the "idea of man" as rational and capable of self-understanding, are conditional and possibly dispensable historical constructs. Foucault refers to his work as archaeology because he seeks to locate these concepts as artifacts of a particular historical formation. However, they are not isolated. Past conceptual structure is a precondition for the present one. Foucault borrows from Nietzsche the term genealogy to describe this phenomenon.

The way we talk about and categorize labor, life, and language in terms of economics, biology, and philology is a mutation of earlier discourse on wealth, natural history, and grammar. The increasingly scientific approach to examining ourselves is reflected in fields such as medicine; doctors focus on the organs and mechanics of the body rather than the whole person, and in society as a whole; the objectification of man influenced the development of the modern state, in which all human activity is politicized. Regarding the body and society as objects to be manipulated and controlled results in standardization and its enforcement through pervasive forms of disciplinary technology.

Classification defines our conceptual framework and denies what fails to fit into it (i.e., in the process of defining sexuality, categories of deviants are created). Attempts at a rational understanding and organization of society, instead of bringing freedom, create victims and new forms of control. Foucault believed that power protects itself by mystifying its control over knowledge and that in general, privileging certain forms of discourse invests them with power that they don't intrinsically have. Recognizing the origin of socially constructed power relations allows an understanding of the limits and dangers of the ways in which we conceive of knowledge and provides a basis from which to reason more critically and freely.

Foucault's philosophy amounts to a theory of language and a vision of the nature of society which is marked more by skepticism than authority and offers a set of tools rather than a program of action. He is less interested in offering truth and more in asking what it means to call something true. His importance lies in his attempt to identify and explain social constructs and challenge accepted truths, such as the faith in scientific and humanitarian progress.

—Katherine Davis

(Summerland, California, 1992)

BOOKS BY MICHEL FOUCAULT

The Archaeology of Knowledge, translated by A.M. Sheridan- Smith. London: Tavistock, 1972 (Translation of L'archeologie du savoir)

ABOUT

Brain, D. (review) CONTEMPORARY SOCIOLOGY 19(6):902-906 November 1990

Brown, B. and Cousins, M. "The Linguistic Fault: The Case of Foucault's Archaeology", ECONOMY AND SOCIETY 9:251-278 1980

Caws, Peter. (review) NEW YORK TIMES BOOK REVIEW October 22, 1972, p6+

Close, Anthony. "Centering the De-Centerers: Foucault and Las Meninas", PHILOSOPHY AND LITERATURE 11(1):21-36 April 1987

Culler, Jonathan. "Language and Knowledge", YALE REVIEW 62:290-296 1972

Deledalle, Gerard. (review) JOURNAL OF THE HISTORY OF PHILOSOPHY 10:495-502 1972

Flynn, Bernard. "Michel Foucault and the Husserlian Problematic of a Transcendental Philosophy of History", PHILOSOPHY TODAY 22:224-238 1978

Gordon, Colin. "Birth of the Subject", RADICAL PHILOSOPHY 17:15-25 1977

Guedon, Jean-Claude. "Michel Foucault: The Knowledge of Power and the Power of Knowledge", BULLETIN OF THE HISTORY OF MEDICINE 51:245-277 1977

Habermas, Jurgen. "Some Questions Concerning the Theory of Power: Foucault Again" in Habermas, Jurgen. The Philosophical Discourse of Modernity. Cambridge: MIT Press, 1987, p266-293

Kermode, Frank. (review) NEW YORK REVIEW OF BOOKS May 1973, p37

Leland, Dorothy. "On Reading and Writing the World: Foucault's History of Thought", CLIO 4:225-243 1975

Luke, Carmen. "Epistemic Rupture and Typography: 'The Archaeology of Knowledge' and 'The Order of Things' Reconsidered", SOCIOLINGUISTICS 17(2):141-155 1988

McDonell, Donald. "On Foucault's Philosophical Method", CANADIAN JOURNAL OF PHILOSOPHY 7:537-553 1977

Megill, Allan. "Foucault, Structuralism and the Ends of History", JOURNAL OF MODERN HISTORY 51:451-503 1979

Minson, Jeff. "Strategies for Socialists?, ECONOMY AND SOCIETY 9:1-43 1980

Poster, Mark. "The Future According to Foucault: The Archaeology of Knowledge and Intellectual History" in LaCapra, Dominick and Kaplan, Steven, eds. Modern European Intellectual History: Reappraisals and New Perspectives. Ithaca, NY: Cornell University Press, 1982, p137-152

Said, Edward. "An Ethics of Language", DIACRITICS 4(2):28-37 1974

_________. "Michel Foucault as an Intellectual Imagination", BOUNDARY 2 1:1-36 1972

Shaffer, Elinor. "The Archaeology of Michel Foucault", STUDIES IN HISTORY AND PHILOSOPHY OF SCIENCE 7(3):269-275 1976

Warren, Neil. (review) SOCIAL SCIENCE AND MEDICINE 7:400-402 1973

The Birth of the Clinic: An Archaeology of Medical Perception, translated by A.M. Sheridan Smith. New York: Pantheon, 1973 (Translation of Naissance de la clinique: une archeologie du regard medical)

ABOUT

Armstrong, D. "The Subject and The Social in Medicine: An Appreciation of Michel Foucault", SOCIOLOGY OF HEALTH AND ILLNESS 7(1):108-117 1985

Aronson, Alfred. "Medicine: History and Theory", YALE REVIEW 63:473-476 1974

Casey, Edward. "The Place of Space in 'The Birth of the Clinic'", JOURNAL OF MEDICINE AND PHILOSOPHY 12:351-356 November 1987

Caws, Peter. "Medical Change", NEW REPUBLIC 10:28-30 November 1973

Figlio, Karl. (review) BRITISH JOURNAL FOR THE HISTORY OF SCIENCE 10:164-167 1977

Hahn, Roger. (review) AMERICAN JOURNAL OF SOCIOLOGY 80:1503-1504 1975

Kaplan, Donald. (review) VILLAGE VOICE November 22, 1973, p29+

Kupers, Terry. (review) SCIENCE AND SOCIETY 39:235-238 1975

Lasch, Christopher. (review) NEW YORK TIMES BOOK REVIEW February 24, 1974, p6

Mainette, Jose. (review) JOURNAL OF MEDICINE AND PHILOSOPHY 2:77-83 1977

Oldman, David. (review) SOCIOLOGY 9:359-360 1975

Ophir, Adi. "Michel Foucault and the Semiotics of the Phenomenal", DIALOGUE 27(3):387-415 Fall 1988

Poynter, F. (review) HISTORY OF SCIENCE 3:140-143 1964

Starobinsky, Jean. (review) NEW YORK REVIEW OF BOOKS 22:18-22 January 1976

<u>Death and the Labyrinth: The World of Raymond Roussel</u>, translated by Charles Ruas. Garden City, NY: Doubleday, 1986 (Translation of <u>Raymond Roussel</u>)

ABOUT

(review) LONDON REVIEW OF BOOKS 9:11 October 15, 1987
Malin, I. (review) REVIEW OF CONTEMPORARY FICTION 7:253 Fall 1987
Pilling, John. "A Little Posthumous Prosperity: Raymond Roussel", PN REVIEW 15(1):43-46 1988
Shiveley, C. (review) GAY COMMUNITY NEWS 14:5 May 10, 1987

<u>Discipline and Punish: The Birth of the Prison</u>, translated by Alan Sheridan. New York: Pantheon, 1977 (Translation of <u>Surveiller et punir: naissance de la prison</u>)

ABOUT

Armstrong, D. "The Subject and the Social in Medicine: An Appreciation of Michel Foucault", SOCIOLOGY OF HEALTH AND ILLNESS 7(1):108-117 1985
Barham, P. (review) SOCIOLOGY 13:111-115 1979
Bersani, Leo. "The Subject of Power", DIACRITICS 7:2-21 1977
Bogard, William. "Discipline and Deterrence: Rethinking Foucault on the Question of Power in Contemporary Society", SOCIAL SCIENCE JOURNAL 28(3):325-346 July 1991
Bove, Paul. "Mendacious Innocents: or, the Modern Genealogist as Conscientious Intellectual: Nietzsche, Foucault, Said", BOUNDARY 2 9(3)/10(1):359-388 1981
_________. "Mendacious Innocents: or, the Modern Genealogist as Conscientious Intellectual: Nietzsche, Foucault, Said" <u>in</u> O'Hara, Daniel, ed. <u>Why Nietzsche Now?</u> Bloomington: Indiana University Press, 1985, p359-388
Bunn, James. (review) STRUCTURALIST REVIEW 1(3):84-91 Summer 1979
Cohen, Stanley. "The Archaeology of Power", CONTEMPORARY SOCIOLOGY 7:566-568 1978
Coles, Robert. "From Torture to Technology", NEW YORKER 54:95-98 January 29, 1979
D'Amico, Robert. (review) TELOS 36:169-183 1978
Di Piero, W. (review) COMMONWEAL 105:313-315 May 12, 1978
Driver, F. "Power, Space and the Body: A Critical Assessment of Foucault", ENVIRONMENT AND PLANNING D 3(4):425-446 1985

Eco, Umberto. "Language, Power, Force" in Eco, Umberto. Travels in Hyperreality: Essays. New York: Harcourt, Brace, Jovanovich, 1986, p239-255

Farganis, James. (review) THEORY AND SOCIETY 10(5):741-745 September 1981

Ferguson, Harvie. (review) INTERNATIONAL JOURNAL OF CRIMINOLOGY AND PENOLOGY 6:269-271 1978

Fine, Bob. "Struggles Against Discipline: The Theory and Politics of Michel Foucault", CAPITAL AND CLASS 9:75-96 1979

Frank. A. "The Politics of the New Positivity", HUMAN STUDIES 5(1):61-67 1982

Garland, David. "Frameworks of Inquiry in the Sociology of Punishment", BRITISH JOURNAL OF SOCIOLOGY 41(1):1-15 March 1990

Geertz, Clifford. "Stir Crazy", NEW YORK REVIEW OF BOOKS January 26, 1978, p4-6

Giddings, Robert. (review) DICKENS STUDIES NEWSLETTER 12(1):19-24 1981

Goldstein, Jan. (review) JOURNAL OF MODERN HISTORY 51:116-118 1979

Goodman, D. (review) CROSS CURRENTS 28:378-382 1978

Gordon, Colin. "Birth of the Subject", RADICAL PHILOSOPHY 17:15-25 1977

Greenberg, D. (review) SOCIOLOGY AND SOCIAL RESEARCH 64:140-143 1979

Hillyard, P. (review) COMMUNITY DEVELOPMENT JOURNAL 14:163-165 1979

Hussain, Athar. (review) SOCIOLOGICAL REVIEW 26:932-939 1978

Ignatieff, M. "State, Civil Society and Total Institutions: A Critique of Recent Social Histories of Punishment" in Tonry, Michael and Morris, Norval, eds. Crime and Justice: Annual Review of Research: Volume 3. Chicago: University of Chicago Press, 1981, p153-192

__________. "State, Civil Society and Total Institutions: A Critique of Recent Social Histories of Punishment" in Cohen, Stanley and Scull, Andrew, eds. Social Control and the State. New York: St. Martin's Press, 1983, p75-105

Kanner, George. "Thinking About Jail", HARVARD CIVIL RIGHTS/CIVIL LIBERTIES LAW REVIEW 13:573-586 1978

Kaplan, Roger. "Jail and Society", COMMENTARY 65(5):82-86 1978

Kurzweil, Edith. "Law and Disorder", PARTISAN REVIEW 44:293-297 1977

Lentricchia, Frank. "Reading Foucault: Punishment, Labor, Resistance", RARITAN 1(4):5-32 1982

Locke, Richard. "In the Cage", NEW YORK TIMES BOOKS REVIEW March 26, 1978, p3

Lucas, Colin. "Power and the Panopticon", TIMES LITERARY SUPPLEMENT September 26, 1975, p1090

Marshall, James. "An Anti-Foundationalist Approach to Discipline and Authority", DISCOURSE 7(2):1-20 April 1987

McConnell, Frank. (review) NEW REPUBLIC 178:32-34 April 1, 1978

Ophir, Adi. "The Semiotics of Power: Reading Michel Foucault's 'Discipline and Punish'", MANUSCRITO 12(2):9-34 October 1989

Paternek, Margaret. "Norms and Normalization: Michel Foucault's Overextended Panoptic Machine", HUMAN STUDIES 10(1):97-121 1987

Rajchman, John. "Nietzsche, Foucault and the Anarchism of Power", SEMIOTEXT(E) 3(1):96-107 1978

Rothman, David. "Society and Its Prisons", NEW YORK TIMES BOOK REVIEW February 19, 1978, p1

Sargent, M. (review) NEW ENGLAND JOURNAL OF PRISON LAW 5:235-240 1979

Sax, Benjamin. "Foucault, Nietzsche, History: Two Modes of the Genealogical Method", HISTORY OF EUROPEAN IDEAS 11:769-781 1989

Seem, Mark. (review) TELOS 29:245-254 1976

Shelley, L. (review) AMERICAN JOURNAL OF SOCIOLOGY 84:1508-1510 179

Singer, R. (review) CRIME AND DELINQUENCY 25:376-379 1979

Sommer, R. (review) CIVIL LIBERTIES REVIEW 5:66-69 1978

Tarbet, Davis. (review) EIGHTEENTH-CENTURY STUDIES 11:509-514 1978

White, Hayden. (review) AMERICAN HISTORICAL REVIEW 82:605-606 1977

Wright, Gordon. "Foucault in Prison", STANFORD FRENCH REVIEW 1:71-78 Spring 1977

Foucault Live: Interviews, 1966-1984, translated by John Johnston. New York: Semiotext(e), 1989 (See Section II for individual interviews)

The Foucault Reader, edited by Paul Rabinow. New York: Pantheon, 1984 (See Section II for individual essays)

ABOUT

(review) ANTIOCH REVIEW 43:253 Spring 1985

(review) SOCIAL FORCES 64:548 December 1985

(review) TIMES EDUCATIONAL SUPPLEMENT July 11, 1986, p23

(review) WILSON QUARTERLY 9:129-130 Summer 1985

Ibde, D. (review) CROSS CURRENTS 35:124-125 Spring 1985

<u>The History of Sexuality, Volume I: An Introduction</u>, translated by Robert Hurley. New York: Pantheon, 1978 (Translation of <u>Histoire de la sexualite, I: la volonte de savoir</u>)

ABOUT

Adamowski, T. "Sex in the Head", CANADIAN FORUM 59:40-42 1979

Amato, J. (review) ANNALS OF THE AMERICAN ACADEMY OF POLITICAL AND SOCIAL SCIENCE 454:239-241 March 1981

Armstrong, D. "The Subject and the Social in Medicine: An Appreciation of Michel Foucault", SOCIOLOGY OF HEALTH AND ILLNESS 7(1):108-117 1985

Bersani, L. "Pedagogy and Pederasty" <u>in</u> Poirier, Richard, ed. <u>Raritan Reading</u>. New Brunswick, NJ: Rutgers University Press, 1990, p1-7

Bevis, Phil and others. "Archaelogizing Genealogy: Michel Foucault and the Economy of Austerity", ECONOMY AND SOCIETY 18(3):323-345 August 1989

Birken, L. (review) TELOS 81:162-171 Fall 1989

Blake, Nancy. "Psychoanalysis and Femininity", STRUCTURALIST REVIEW 1(2):90-96 1978

Bordo, S. (review) CROSS CURRENTS 30:194-197 1980

Bounds, Elizabeth. (review) UNION SEMINARY QUARTERLY REVIEW 41(3/4):107-113 1987

Colburn, Kenneth, jr. "Desire and Discourse in Foucault: The Sign of the Fig Leaf in Michelangelo's David", HUMAN STUDIES 10(1):61-79 1987

D'Amico, Robert. (review) TELOS 36:169-183 1978

Earle, William. "Foucault's 'The Use of Pleasure' as Philosophy", METAPHILOSOPHY 20:169-177 April 1989

Eco, Umberto. "Language, Power, Force" <u>in</u> Eco, Umberto. <u>Travels in Hyperreality: Essays</u>. New York: Harcourt, Brace, Jovanovich, 1986, p239-255

Gilbert, Arthur. (review) AMERICAN HISTORICAL REVIEW 84:1020-1021 1979

Goodheart, Eugene. "Desire and Its Discontents", PARTISAN REVIEW 55(3):387-403 Summer 1988

Gordon, Colin. "Birth of the Subject", RADICAL PHILOSOPHY 17:15-25 1977

Guedon, Jean-Claude. (review) INTERNATIONAL JOURNAL OF LAW AND PSYCHIATRY 1:105-107 1978

Halperin, David. "Is There a History of Sexuality?" HISTORY AND THEORY 28(3):257-274 October 1989

Harkness, James. "Sex, Race and Age", SOCIETY 16(6):82-86 1979
Kurzweil, Edith. (review) THEORY AND SOCIETY 8:422-425 1979
_________. "Michel Foucault's History of Sexuality as Interpreted by Feminists and Marxists", SOCIAL RESEARCH 53(4):647-663 Winter 1986
La Fountain, Marc. "Foucault and Dr. Ruth", CRITICAL STUDIES IN MASS COMMUNICATION 6(2):123-137 June 1989
La Grand, Eva. (review) STRUCTURALIST REVIEW 1(3):104-106 1979
Lasch, Christopher. "Life in the Therapeutic State", NEW YORK REVIEW OF BOOKS June 12, 1980, p24-32
Levine, David. "The F-Word: Foucault's History of Sexuality", INTERNATIONAL LABOR AND WORKING-CLASS HISTORY 41:42-48 Spring 1992
Pollis, Carol. "The Apparatus of Sexuality: Reflections on Foucault's Contributions to the Study of Sex in History", JOURNAL OF SEX RESEARCH 23(3):401-408 August 1987
Rediker, M. (review) WILLIAM AND MARY QUARTERLY 36:637-640 1979
Richlin, A. "Zeus and Metis, Foucault, Feminism, Classics", HELOS 18(2):160-180 Fall 1991
Shaffer, Elinor. (review) SIGNS 5:812-820 1980
Smart, Barry. (review) BOUNDARY 2 18(1):201-225 Spring 1991
Taylor, Charles. "Foucault on Freedom and Truth" in Taylor, Charles. Philosophy and the Human Sciences. Cambridge: Cambridge University Press, 1985, p152-184
Vicinus, M. (review) FEMINIST STUDIES 8:133-156 Spring 1982
Vine, Richard. "The History of an Illusion", GEORGIA REVIEW 33:918-922 1979
White, Hayden. "The Archaeology of Sex", TIMES LITERARY SUPPLEMENT May 6, 1977, p565
Wilson, Emmett, Jr. (review) JOURNAL OF THE AMERICAN PSYCHOANALYTIC ASSOCIATION 30(3):797-799 1982
Zinner, Jacqueline. (review) TELOS 36:215-225 1978

The History of Sexuality: Volume II: The Use of Pleasure, translated by Robert Hurley. New York: Pantheon, 1985 (Translation of Histoire de la sexualite, II: L'usage de plaisirs)

ABOUT

Bersani, L. "Pedagogy and Pederasty" in Poirier, Richard, ed. Raritan Reading. New Brunswick: Rutgers University Press, 1990, p1-7
Bevis, Phil and others. "Archaelogizing Genealogy: Michel Foucault and the Economy of Austerity", ECONOMY AND SOCIETY 18(3):323-345 August 1989

Blair, Carole. (review) PHILOSOPHY AND RHETORIC 21(3):237-240 1988
Brain, D. (review) CONTEMPORARY SOCIOLOGY 19(6):902-906 November 1990
Bulough, L. (review) AMERICAN HISTORICAL REVIEW 90:387-388 April 1985
Callinicos, A. "Foucault's Third Theoretical Displacement", THEORY, CULTURE AND SOCIETY 3(3):171+ 1986
Cameron, A. (review) JOURNAL OF ROMAN STUDIES 76:266-271 1986
Diprose, R. "The Use of Pleasure in Constitution of Body", AUSTRALIAN FEMINIST STUDIES 5:94+ Summer 1987
Eco, Umberto. "Language, Power, Force" in Eco, Umberto. Travels in Hyperreality: Essays. New York: Harcourt, Brace, Jovanovich, 1986, p239-255
Edmunds, Lowell. "Foucault and Theognis", CLASSICAL AND MODERN LITERATURE: A QUARTERLY 8(2):79-91 Winter 1988
Gibb, H. (review) AUSTRALIAN JOURNAL OF PSYCHOLOGY 42(3):338-339 December 1990
Goodheart, Eugene. "Desire and Its Discontents", PARTISAN REVIEW 55(3):387-403 Summer 1988
Halperin, David. "Is There a History of Sexuality?" HISTORY AND THEORY 28(3):257-274 October 1989
__________. "Sexual Ethics and Technologies of the Self in Classical Greece", AMERICAN JOURNAL OF PHILOLOGY 107:274-286 Summer 1986
Harrison, Paul. "From Bodies to Ethics", THESIS ELEVEN 16:128-140 1987
Ingatieff, Michael. (review) TIMES LITERARY SUPPLEMENT September 28, 1984, p1071-1072
Kurzweil, Edith. "Michel Foucault's History of Sexuality as Interpreted by Feminists and Marxists", SOCIAL RESEARCH 53(4):647-663 Winter 1986
Lefkowitz, M. (review) PARTISAN REVIEW 52(4):460-466 1985
Levine, David. "The F-Word: Foucault's History of Sexuality", INTERNATIONAL LABOR AND WORKING-CLASS HISTORY 41:42-48 Spring 1992
Lloyd, G. "The Mind on Sex" NEW YORK REVIEW OF BOOKS 33(4):24-28 March 13, 1986
McL Currie, H. (review) THEORY, CULTURE AND SOCIETY 3(3):189+ 1986
Nussbaum, Martha. (review) NEW YORK TIMES BOOK REVIEW November 10, 1985, p13+

Olivier, L. (review) CANADIAN JOURNAL OF POLITICAL SCIENCE 18:839-842 December 1985
Richlin, A. "Zeus and Metis, Foucault, Feminism, Classics", HELOS 18(2):160-180 Fall 1991
Shively, C. (review) GAY COMMUNITY NEWS 13(50):S1+ July 6, 1986
Smart, Barry. "On the Subjects of Sexuality, Ethics and Politics in the Work of Foucault", BOUNDARY 2 18(1):201-225 Spring 1991
Steiner, G. (review) NEW YORKER 62:105 March 17, 1986

<u>The History of Sexuality: Volume III: The Care of the Self</u>. New York: Pantheon Books, 1986 (Translation of <u>Histoire de la sexualite: III. le souci de soi</u>)

ABOUT

Bersani, L. "Pedagogy and Pederasty" <u>in</u> Poirier, Richard, ed. <u>Raritan Reading</u>. New Brunswick, NJ: Rutgers University Press, 1990, p1-7
Bevis, Phil and others. "Archaelogizing Genealogy: Michel Foucault and the Economy of Austerity", ECONOMY AND SOCIETY 18(3):323-345 August 1989
Boswell, J. (review) NEW YORK TIMES BOOK REVIEW January 18, 1987, p31
Brain, D. (review) CONTEMPORARY SOCIOLOGY 19(6):902-906 November 1990
Callinicos, A. "Foucault's Third Theoretical Displacement", THEORY, CULTURE AND SOCIETY 3(3):171+ 1986
Cameron, A. (review) JOURNAL OF ROMAN STUDIES 76:266-271 1986
Eco, Umberto. "Language, Power, Force" <u>in</u> Eco, Umberto. <u>Travels in Hyperreality: Essays</u>. New York: Harcourt, Brace, Jovanovich, 1986, p239-255
Goodheart, Eugene. "Desire and Its Discontents", PARTISAN REVIEW 55(3):387-403 Summer 1988
Gordon, C. "Life like a Human" NEW STATESMAN AND SOCIETY 115:22-23 May 6, 1988
Halperin, David. "Is There a History of Sexuality?" HISTORY AND THEORY 28(3):257-274 October 1989
Harrison, Paul. "From Bodies to Ethics", THESIS ELEVEN 16:128-140 1987
Kimmel, M. (review) PSYCHOLOGY TODAY 21:68-69 October 1987
Kurzweil, Edith. "Michel Foucault's History of Sexuality as Interpreted by Feminists and Marxists", SOCIAL RESEARCH 53(4):647-663 Winter 1986
Lefkowitz, M. (review) PARTISAN REVIEW 52(4):460 1986

Levine, David. "The F-Word: Foucault's History of Sexuality", INTERNATIONAL LABOR AND WORKING-CLASS HISTORY 41:42-48 Spring 1992

Marin, R. (review) COMMENTARY 84:63-65 July 1987

Olivier, L. (review) CANADIAN JOURNAL OF POLITICAL SCIENCE 18:839-842 December 1985

Porter, Ray. "Sex in the Head", LONDON REVIEW OF BOOKS 10(13):13-14 July 7, 1988

Richlin, A. "Zeus and Metis, Foucault, Feminism, Classics", HELOS 18(2):160-180 Fall 1991

Smart, Barry. "On the Subjects of Sexuality, Ethics and Politics in the Work of Foucault", BOUNDARY 2 18(1):201-225 Spring 1991

Williams, S. (review) AUSTRALIAN PSYCHOLOGIST 27(2):132 July 1992

I, Pierre Riviere, Having Slaughtered My Mother, My Sister, and My Brother...: A Case of Parricide in the 19th Century, translated by Frank Jellinek. New York: Pantheon Books, 1975 (edited by Michel Foucault) (Translation of Moi, Pierre Riviere, ayant egorge ma mere, ma soeur et mon frere...un cas de parricide au XIXe siecle)

ABOUT

Bittner, E. (review) AMERICAN JOURNAL OF SOCIOLOGY 82:256-260 1976

Cobb, Richard. (review) NEW SOCIETY 44:550-552 1978

Da Feo, Ronald. "Anatomy of A Murder", NATIONAL REVIEW 27:950-951 August 29, 1975

Delany, Paul. (review) NEW YORK TIMES BOOK REVIEW May 18, 1975, p31-32

Gordon, Colin. "Nasty Tales", RADICAL PHILOSOPHY 15:31-32 1976

Klee, Earl. (review) JOURNAL OF THE HISTORY OF THE BEHAVIORAL SCIENCES 12:192-194 1976

Macdonald, John. (review) AMERICAN JOURNAL OF PSYCHIATRY 132:1336 1975

Marshall, Donald. "Writer's Choice", PARTISAN REVIEW 43:489-490 1976

Muggeridge, Malcolm. "Milne and Manson: Two Styles of Fantasy", ESQUIRE 84:23+ July 1975

Sadoff, Robert. "Parricide: The Search for Motivation", CONTEMPORARY PSYCHOLOGY 21:440-441 1976

Tennessen, Carol. "Nothing But the Truth: The Case of Pierre Riviere", UNIVERSITY OF TORONTO QUARTERLY 57(2):290-305 Winter 1987/88

Language, Counter-Memory, Practice: Selected Essays and Interviews, translated by Donald Bouchard and Sherry Simon. Ithaca, NY: Cornell University Press, 1977 (See Section II for individual essays and interviews)

ABOUT

Barouw, Jeffrey. (review) REVIEW OF METAPHYSICS 32(4):750-752 June 1979

Chua, Beng-Huat. (review) CONTEMPORARY SOCIOLOGY 8:318-319 1979

D'Amico, Robert. (review) TELOS 36:169-183 1978

Good, G. (review) CANADIAN LITERATURE 82:102-104 1979

Judovitz, Dalia. (review) MODERN LANGUAGE NOTES 93:755-778 1978

Leaman, A. (review) ENVIRONMENT AND PLANNING 11:1079-1082 1979

Mall, James. (review) JOURNAL OF AESTHETICS AND ART CRITICISM 37:369-372 1979

Meisel, Perry. "What Foucault Knows", SALMAGUNDI 44/45:235-241 1979

Omera, M. (review) SUB-STANCE 21:160 1978

Prince, Gerald. (review) CRITICISM 20:324-325 1978

Radway, Janice. (review) SOUTHERN HUMANITIES REVIEW 13:266-267 1979

Richmond, Sheldon. (review) PHILOSOPHY OF THE SOCIAL SCIENCES 15:369-371 September 1985

Riddel, Joseph. "Re-Doubling the Commentary", CONTEMPORARY LITERATURE 29:237-250 1979

Schier, Donald. "Thought as Destruction", CARLETON MISCELLANY 18:175-179 1980

Madness and Civilization: A History of Insanity in the Age of Reason, translated by Richard Howard. New York: Pantheon, 1965 (Translation of Folie et deraison: histoire de la folie a l'age classique)

ABOUT

Armstrong, D. "The Subject and the Social in Medicine: An Appreciation of Michel Foucault", SOCIOLOGY OF HEALTH AND ILLNESS 7(1):108-117 1985

Brain, D. (review) CONTEMPORARY SOCIOLOGY 19(6):902-906 November 1990

Burnham, John. (review) JOURNAL OF NERVOUS AND MENTAL DISORDERS 143:455-457 1966

Cauthen, Nelson. (review) HUMAN CONTEXT 7:628-631 1975

Cook, Deborah. "Madness and the Cogito: Derrida's Critique of 'Folie et Deraison'", JOURNAL OF THE BRITISH SOCIETY FOR PHENOMENOLOGY 21(2):164-174 May 1990

Dumont, Matthew. "What is Madness?", SOCIAL SCIENCE AND MEDICINE 2:502-504 1968

Felman, Shoshana. "Madness and Philosophy or Literature's Reason", YALE FRENCH STUDIES 52:206-208 1975

Gay, Peter. "Chains and Couches", COMMENTARY 40(4):93-95 1965

Gearhart, Suzanne. "Establishing Rationality in the Historical Text: Foucault and the Problem of Unreason" in Gearhart, Suzanne. The Open Boundary of History and Fiction: A Critical Approach to the French Enlightenment. Princeton: Princeton University Press, 1984, p29-56

Howard, Richard. (review) TIMES LITERARY SUPPLEMENT October 6, 1961, p653-654

Ingleby, D. "Mental Health and Social Order" in Cohen, Stanley and Scull, Andrew, eds. Social Control and the State. New York: St. Martin's Press, 1983, p141-188

Laing, R. "Sanity and Madness: The Invention of Madness", NEW STATESMAN 73:843 June 16, 1967

Marcus, Steven. "In Praise of Folly", NEW YORK REVIEW OF BOOKS November 3, 1966, p6+

Matza, David. (review) AMERICAN SOCIOLOGICAL REVIEW 31:551-552 1966

Midelfort, H. "Madness and Civilization in Early Modern Europe: A Reappraisal of Michel Foucault" in Malament, Barbara, ed. After the Reformation, Essays in Honor of J.H. Hexter. Philadelphia: University of Pennsylvania Press, 1980, p247-265

Paulson, Ronald. (review) JOURNAL OF ENGLISH AND GERMANIC PHILOLOGY 67:161-165 1968

Peters, Michael. (review) SOCIOLOGICAL REVIEW 19:634-638 1971

Rieff, Philip. (review) ANNALS OF THE AMERICAN ACADEMY OF SOCIAL AND POLITICAL SCIENCES 371:258-259 1967

Rose, Nikolas. "Of Madness Itself: 'Histoire de la folie' and the Object of Psychiatric History", HISTORY OF THE HUMAN SCIENCES 3(3):373-380 October 1990

Rousseau, G. (review) EIGHTEENTH-CENTURY STUDIES 4:90-95 1970

Scalzo, Joseph. "Campanella, Foucault and Madness in Late-Sixteenth Century Italy", THE SIXTEENTH CENTURY JOURNAL 21(3):360-371 Fall 1990

Sedgwick, Peter. "Michel Foucault: The Anti-History of Psychiatry" in Psycho Politics: Laing, Foucault, Goffman, Szasz and the Future of Mass Psychiatry. New York: Harper, 1982, p125-148

Simon, John. (review) MODERN LANGUAGE NOTES 78:85-88 1963

Strong, Beret. "Foucault, Freud and French Feminism: Theorizing Hysteria as Theorizing the Feminine", LITERATURE AND PSYCHOLOGY 35(4):10-26 1989

Mental Illness and Psychology, translated by Alan Sheridan. New York: Harper and Row, 1976 (Translation of Maladie mentale et personnalite)

The Order of Things: An Archaeology of the Human Sciences. London: Tavistock, 1970 (Translation of Les mots et les choses: une archeologie des sciences humaines)

ABOUT

Caws, Peter. "Language as the Human Reality", NEW REPUBLIC 164:28 March 27, 1971

Culler, Jonathan. (review) CAMBRIDGE REVIEW 93:104-105 January 29, 1971

Flynn, Bernard. "Michel Foucault and the Husserlian Problematic of a Transcendental Philosophy of History", PHILOSOPHY TODAY 22:224-238 1978

Funt, David. "The Structuralist Debate", HUDSON REVIEW 22(4):623-646 1969/70

Gordon, Colin. "Birth of the Subject", RADICAL PHILOSOPHY 17:15-25 1977

Habermas, Jurgen. "Some Questions Concerning the Theory of Power: Foucault Again" in Habermas, Jurgen. The Philosophical Discourse of Modernity. Cambridge: MIT Press, 1987, p266-293

Hacking, Ian. "Michel Foucault's Immature Science", NOUS 13:39-51 1979

Harding, D. (review) NEW YORK REVIEW OF BOOKS 18:21-22 August 12, 1972

Howard, Richard. "Our Sense of Where We Are", NATION 213:21-22 July 5, 1971

Leland, Dorothy. "On Reading and Writing the World: Foucault's History of Thought", CLIO 4:225-243 1975

Luke, Carmen. "Epistemic Rupture and Typography: 'The Archaeology of Knowledge' and 'The Order of Things' Reconsidered", SOCIOLINGUISTICS 17(2):141-155 1988

Megill, Allan. "Foucault, Structuralism and the Ends of History", JOURNAL OF MODERN HISTORY 51:451-503 1979

Moore, John. (review) SCIENCE AND SOCIETY 35:490-494 1971

Ophir, Adi. "Michel Foucault and the Semiotics of the Phenomenal", DIALOGUE 27(3):387-415 Fall 1988

Racevskis, Karlis. "The Conative Function of the Other in 'Les Mots et Les Choses'", REVUE INTERNATIONALE DE PHILOSOPHIE 44(173):231-240 1990

Rousseau, G. "Whose Enlightenment? Not Man's: The Case of Michel Foucault", EIGHTEENTH-CENTURY STUDIES 6:238-256 1972/73

Said, Edward. "An Ethics of Language", DIACRITICS 4(2):28-37 1974

Snyder, Joel. "Las Meninas and the Mirror of the Prince", CRITICAL INQUIRY 11(4):539-572 June 1985

Weightman, John. "On Not Understanding Michel Foucault", AMERICAN SCHOLAR 58(3):383-406 Summer 1989

White, Hayden. "Foucault Decoded: Notes from Underground", HISTORY AND THEORY 12:23-54 1973

Politics, Philosophy, Culture: Interviews and Other Writings, 1977-1984, translated by Alan Sheridan and others. New York: Routledge, 1988 (See Section II for individual essays and interviews)

ABOUT

(review) ETHICS 100:907 July 1990

(review) RELIGIOUS STUDIES REVIEW 15:239 July 1989

Boire, Gary. (review) CANADIAN LITERATURE 128:141-143 Spring 1991

Bowen, J. (review) SOCIOLOGICAL REVIEW 38(2):364-366 May 1990

Buss, Robin. "An Intellectual Keen on Prisons", INDEPENDENT 683:26 December 17, 1988

Dumm, Thomas. (review) SOCIOLOGY 23(3):495-496 August 1989

Latane, David. "At Play in the Field of Foucault: A Review of Some Recent Texts", CRITICAL TEXTS 6:39-58 1989

McDonald, Briget. (review) MODERN LANGUAGE NOTES 104(4):945-949 September 1989

McWhorter, Ladelle. (review) CANADIAN PHILOSOPHICAL REVIEWS 10(9):352-356 September 1990

Moi, Toril. (review) FRENCH STUDIES 44(3):370-371 July 1990

Oldfield, P. (review) NEW STATESMAN AND SOCIETY 1:43 November 18, 1988

Roth, M. (review) AMERICAN HISTORICAL REVIEW 95(3):776-777 June 1990

Tester, K. (review) SOCIOLOGY 25:158-159 February 1991

Power/Knowledge: Selected Interviews and Other Writings, 1972-1977, translated by Colin Gordon, Leo Marshall, John Mepham and Kate Soper. New York: Pantheon Books, 1980 (See Section II for individual essays and interviews)

ABOUT

Bernauer, J. (review) INTERNATIONAL PHILOSOPHICAL QUARTERLY 22:87-95 March 1982

Brain, D. (review) CONTEMPORARY SOCIOLOGY 19(6):902-906 November 1990

Caldwell, N. (review) CROSS CURRENTS 32:495-498 Winter 1982/83

Dews, Peter. (review) NEW STATESMEN 101:20-21 January 2, 1981

Gordon, Colin. "Afterword" in Power/Knowledge: Selected Interviews and Other Writings. New York: Pantheon Books, 1980
Hacking, Ian. "The Archaeology of Foucault", NEW YORK REVIEW OF BOOKS 28:32-37 May 14, 1981
Marshall, James. "Foucault and Education", AUSTRALIAN JOURNAL OF EDUCATION 33(2):99-113 August 1989
Rorty, Richard. "Beyond Nietzsche and Marx", LONDON REVIEW OF BOOKS 3:5-6 February 19, 1981
Taylor, Charles. "Foucault on Freedom and Truth" in Taylor, Charles. Philosophy and the Human Sciences. Cambridge: Cambridge University Press, 1985, p152-184
Taylor, Laurie. (review) NEW SOCIETY 54:182+ October 23, 1980

Remarks on Marx: Conversations with Duccio Trombadori, translated by R. Goldstein and James Cascaito. New York: Semiotext(e), 1991 (See Section II for individual interviews)

This is Not a Pipe, translated by James Harkness. Berkeley: University of California Press, 1981 (Translation of Ceci n'est pas une pipe: deux lettres et quartre dessins de Rene Magritte)

ABOUT

Levy, Silvano. "Foucault on Magritte on Resemblance", MODERN LANGUAGE REVIEW 85(1):50-56 January 1990
Margolis, Joseph. (review) JOURNAL OF AESTHETICS AND ART CRITICISM 43:224-225 Winter 1984
McEvilley, T. (review) ARTFORUM 22:68 October 1983
Phillips, A. (review) TIMES LITERARY SUPPLEMENT April 27, 1984, p475
Turner, B. "Foucault and the Crisis of Modernity", THEORY, CULTURE AND SOCIETY 3(3):179+ 1986
Van De Pitte, Margaret. (review) DIALOGUE 24:742-745 Winter 1985
Van Morstein, Petra. (review) CANADIAN PHILOSOPHICAL REVIEW 4:144-47 August 1984
Weil, J. (review) ETC. 40:124-126 Spring 1983
Wolff, Janet. (review) BRITISH JOURNAL OF AESTHETICS 24:368-370 Autumn 1984

BOOKS IN FRENCH

L'archeologie du savoir. Paris: Editions Gallimard, 1969 (Translated into English as The Archaeology of Knowledge)

Ceci n'est pas une pipe: deux lettres et quartre dessins de Rene Magritte. Montpeltier: Fata Morgana, 1973 (Translated into English as This is Not a Pipe)

Le Desordre des familles. Paris: Gallimard, 1982

Folie et deraison: histoire de la folie a l'age classique. Paris: Librairie Plon, 1961 (Translated into English as Madness and Civilization: A History of Insanity in the Age of Reason)

Histoire de la sexualite, I: la volonte de savoir. Paris: Gallimard, 1976 (Translated into English as The History of Sexuality, Volume I: An Introduction)

Histoire de la sexualite, II: L'usage de plaisirs. Paris: Gallimard, 1984 (Translated into English as The History of Sexuality, Volume 2: The Use of Pleasure)

Histoire de la sexualite, III: Le Souci de soi. Paris: Gallimard, 1984 (Translated into English as The History of Sexuality, Volume 3: The Care of the Self)

Les Machines a querir. Paris: Institut de l'environnement, 1976

Maladie mentale et personnalite. Paris: Presses Universitaires de France, 1954 (Translated into English as Mental Illness and Psychology)

Masses et politique. Paris: Editions du Centre national de la recherche scientifique, 1988

Moi, Pierre Riviere, ayant egorge ma mere, ma soeur et mon frere...un cas de parricide au XIXe siecle. Paris: Gallimard, 1973 (Translated into English as I, Pierre Riviere, Having Slaughtered My Mother, My Sister and My Brother...: A Case of Parricide in the 19th Century)

Les mots et les choses: une archeologie des sciences humaines. Paris: Gallimard, 1966 (Translated into English as The Order of Things: An Archaeology of the Human Sciences)

Naissance de la clinique: une archeologie du regard medical. Paris: Presses Universitaires de France, 1963 (Translated into English as The Birth of the Clinic: An Archaeology of Medical Perception)

La pensee du dehors. Paris: Fata Morgana, 1986 69p

Raymond Roussel. Paris: Editions Gallimard, 1963 (Translated into English as Death and the Labyrinth: The World of Raymond Roussel)

Resume des cours, 1970-1982. Paris: Gulliard, 1989

ABOUT

Polan, D. (review) SUB-STANCE 61:108-109 1990

Sept propos sur le septieme ange. Saint-Clement: Fata Morgana, 1986 57p

Surveiller et punir: naissance de la prison. Paris: Gallimard, 1975 (Translated into English as Discipline and Punish: The Birth of the Prison)

Theorie d'ensemble. Paris: Editions du Seiul, 1968

La volonte de Savoir. Paris: Gallimard, 1976

ESSAYS BY FOUCAULT

1. **About the Concept of the "Dangerous Individual" in 19th Century Legal Psychiatry**
   in INTERNATIONAL JOURNAL OF LAW AND PSYCHIATRY 1:1-18 1978
   in Politics, Philosophy, Culture* 1988, p125-151
2. **Archaeology of Knowledge** (introduction to Archaeology of Knowledge*)
   in SOCIAL SCIENCE INFORMATION 9(1):175-185 1970
3. **The Art of Telling the Truth** (MAGAZINE LITTERAIRE 207:35-39 May 1984)
   in Politics, Philosophy, Culture* 1988, p86-95
4. **The Battle for Chastity** ("Sexualties occidentales", COMMUNICATIONS Volume 35 1982)
   in Aries, Philippe and Bejin, Andre, eds. Western Sexuality: Practice and Precept in Past and Present Times. London: Blackwell, 1985, p14-25
   in Politics, Philosophy, Culture* 1988, p227-241
5. **Behind the Fable**
   in CRITICAL TEXTS 5:1-5 1988
6. **The Birth of the Asylum** (excerpt from Folie et deraison*)
   in The Foucault Reader* 1984, p141-168
7. **The Body of the Condemned** (excerpt from Surveiller et punir*)
   in The Foucault Reader* 1984, p170-178
8. **The Carceral** (exerpt from Surveiller et punir*)
   in The Foucault Reader* 1984, p234-238
9. **The Catch-All Strategy** (LE NOUVEL OBSERVATEUR 759:57 1979)
   in INTERNATIONAL JOURNAL OF THE SOCIOLOGY OF LAW 16(2):159-162 1988
10. **Complete and Austere Institutions** (excerpt from Surveiller et punir*)
    in The Foucault Reader* 1984, p214-225
11. **The Confession of the Flesh** ("Le jeu de Michel Foucault", ORNICAR 10 1977) (a conversation with Alain Grosrichard and others)
    in Power/Knowledge* 1980, P194-228
12. **Contemporary Music and the Public** (discussion with Pierre Boulez) (CNAC MAGAZINE Volume 15 May/June 1983)
    in PERSPECTIVES OF NEW MUSIC 24:6-12 Fall/Winter 1985
    in Politics, Philosophy, Culture* 1988, p314-322
13. **Cuvier's Position in the History of Biology** ("La Situation de Cuvier dans l'histoire de la biologie", REVUE D'HISTOIRE DES SCIENCES 23:63-69 1970)
    in CRITIQUE OF ANTHROPOLOGY 4:125-130 1979

14. Docile Bodies (excerpt from Surveiller et punir*)
in The Foucault Reader* 1984, p179-187

15. Dream and Existence
in REVIEW OF EXISTENTIAL PSYCHOLOGY AND PSYCHIATRY 19(1):29-78 1984/85
in Hoeller, Keith, ed. Dream and Existence. Seattle: Review of Existential Psychology and Psychiatry, 1986

16. Experiences of Madness (excerpt from Histoire de la folie a l'age classique*)
in HISTORY OF THE HUMAN SCIENCES 4(1):1-25 February 1991

17. The Eye of Power ("L'oeil du pouvoir" in Bentham, Jeremy. Le Panoptique. Paris: Pierre Belfund, 1977) (a conversation with Jean-Pierre Barou and Michelle Perrot)
in SEMIOTEXT(E) 3(2):6-19 1979
in Power/Knowledge* 1980, p146-165

18. Fantasia of the Library ("Un 'fantastique de bibliotheque'", CAHIERS DE LA COMPAGNIE MADELEINE RENAUD-JEAN LOUIS BARRAULT 59:7-30 1967
in Language, Counter-Memory, Practice* 1977, p87-109

19. The Father's No ("Le 'non' du pere", CRITIQUE 178:195-209 1962)
in Language, Counter-Memory, Practice* 1977, p69-86

20. Georges Canuilheim - Philosopher of Error
in IDEOLOGY AND CONSCIOUSNESS 7:51-62 1980

21. Governmentality (Lecture delivered at the College de France, February 1978)
in IDEOLOGY AND CONSCIOUSNESS 6:5-21 1979
in Burchall, Graham and others, eds. The Foucault Effect: Studies in Governmentality. London: Harvester Wheatsheaf, 1991, p87-104

22. The Great Confinement (excerpt from Folie et deraison*)
in The Foucault Reader* 1984, p124-140

23. Grey Mornings of Tolerance
in STANFORD ITALIAN REVIEW 2(2):72-74 Fall 1982

24. History, Discourse and Discontinuity ("Response a une question", ESPRIT 36:8850-8874 1968)
in SALMAGUNDI 20:225-248 Summer/Fall 1972
in Boyers, Robert, ed. Psychological Man. New York: Harper Books, 1975, p208-231
in IDEOLOGY AND CONSCIOUSNESS 3:7-26 Spring 1978 (entitled "Politics and the Study of Discourse")
in Burchall, Graham and others, eds. The Foucault Effect: Studies in Governmentality. London: Harvester Wheatsheaf, 1991, p53-72 (entitled "Politics and the Study of Discourse")

25. History of Systems of Thought (Summary of a course given at the College de France, 1970-71)
in Language, Counter-Memory, Practice* 1977, p199-204

26. **Human Nature: Justice Versus Power**
in Elders, Fons, ed. Reflexive Water: The Basic Concerns of Mankind. London: Souvenir Press, 1974, p135-197

27. **Illegalities and Delinquency** (excerpt from Surveiller et punir*)
in The Foucault Reader* 1984, p226-233

28. **The Intellectuals and Power** (discussion with Gilles Deleuze) ("Les intellectuels et le pouvoir", ARC 49:3-10 1972)
in TELOS 16:103-109 1973
in Language, Counter-Memory, Practice* 1977, p205-217
in Ferguson, Russell and others, eds. Discourses: Conversations in Postmodern Art and Culture. New York; The New Museum of Contemporary Art, 1990, p9-16

29. **Interview**
in TELOS 32:159+ Summer 1977
in THREE PENNY REVIEW 1(1):4-5 1980
in HISTORY OF THE PAST February 1985, p3+

30. **Interview (Speigel interview)** ("Ein gewaltiges Erstauenen", DER SPIEGEL 30:264 October 1978)
in NEW GERMAN CRITIQUE 16:155-156 1979

31. **Interview: Adorno, Horkheimer and Marcuse: Who is a "Negator" of History?** (with Duccio Trombadori)
in Remarks on Marx* 1991, p115-130

32. **Interview: An Aesthetics of Existence** (LE MONDE AUJOURD'HUI April 15-16, 1984)
in Politics, Philosophy, Culture* 1988, p47-53
in Foucault Live* 1989, p309-316

33. **Interview: An Ethics of Pleasure**
in Foucault Live* 1989, p257-277

34. **Interview: An Historian of Culture** ("Un Dibattito Foucault-Preti", IL BIMESTREIN 1973)
in Foucault Live* 1989, p73-88

35. **Interview: Between "Words" and "Things" During May '68** (with Duccio Trombadori)
in Remarks on Marx* 1991, p131-146

36. **Interview: Body/Power** ("Pouvoir et corps", QUEL CORPS? September/October 1975)
in Power/Knowledge* 1980, p55-62

37. **Interview: "But Structuralism Was Not a French Invention"** (with Duccio Trombadori)
in Remarks on Marx* 1991, p83-114

38. **Interview: Clarifications on the Question of Power** (AUT AUT 167/168 1978)
in Foucault Live* 1989, p179-192

39. **Interview: Confinement, Psychiatry, Prison** ("La Folie encerclee", CHANGE 32/33:76-110 1977)
   in Politics, Philosophy, Culture* 1988, p178-210

40. **Interview: Film and Popular Memory** ("Entretien avec Michel Foucault", CAHIERS DU CINEMA 251/252:5-15 July/August 1974)
   in EDINBURGH '77 MAGAZINE Volume 2, 1975
   in RADICAL PHILOSOPHY 11:24-29 1975
   in Foucault Live* 1989, p89-106

41. **Interview: Foucault Responds to Sartre** (LA QUINZAINE LITTERAIRE March 1-15, 1968)
   in Foucault Live* 1989, p35-43

42. **Interview: Friendship as a Lifestyle** (LE GAI PIED April 1981
   in Foucault Live* 1989, p203-209

43. **Interview: History of Sexuality (with Lucette Finas)** ("Michel Foucault: 'le rapports de pouvoir passent a l'interieur des corps", QUINZAINE LITTERAIRE 247:4-6 1977)
   in Morris, Meaghan and Patton, Paul, eds. Michel Foucault: Power, Truth and Strategy. Sydney: Feral Publications, 1979, p67-75
   in Power/Knowledge* 1980, p183-193

44. **Interview: How an "Experience-Book" is Born** (with Duccio Trombadori)
   in Remarks on Marx* 1991, p25-42

45. **Interview: How Much Does It Cost to Tell the Truth** (SPUREN May 1983, June 1983)
   in Foucault Live* 1989, p233-256

46. **Interview: I, Pierre Riviere..."** (CAHIERS DU CINEMA November 1976)
   in Foucault Live* 1989, p131-136

47. **Interview: Iran: The Spirit of a World Without Spirit** (Briere, Claire and Blanchet, Pierre. Iran: la revolution au nom de Dieu. Paris: Seuil, 1979, p227-241)
   in Politics, Philosophy, Culture* 1988, p211-224
   Related Articles
   Stauth, Georg. "Revolution in Spiritless Times: An Essay on Michel Foucault's Enquiries into the Iranian Revolution", INTERNATIONAL SOCIOLOGY 6(3):259-280 September 1991

48. **Interview: Is It Really Important to Think**
   in PHILOSOPHY AND SOCIAL CRITICISM 9(1):29-40 1982
   in Politics, Philosophy, Culture* 1988, p152-156 (entitled "Practicing Criticism")

49. **Interview: On Attica**
   in TELOS 19:154-161 Spring 1974
   in SOCIAL JUSTICE 18(3):26-34 Fall 1991 No. 45

50. **Interview: On Power** (L'EXPRESS July 6-12, 1984, p56-68)
   in Politics, Philosophy, Culture* 1988, p96-109

51. Interview: On the Genealogy of Ethics: An Overview of Work in Progress
- in Dreyfus, Hubert and Rabinow, Paul. Michel Foucault: Beyond Structuralism and Hermeneutics. Chicago: University of Chicago Press, 1983, p229+
- in The Foucault Reader* 1984, p340-372

52. Interview: Polemics, Politics and Problemizations
- in The Foucault Reader* 1984, p381+

53. Interview: Politics and Ethics (based on an unpublished French manuscript)
- in The Foucault Reader* 1984, p373-380

54. Interview: Power and Sex ("Foucault: Non au sexe roi", NOUVEL OBSERVATEUR March 12, 1977, p92+)
- in TELOS 32:152-161 Summer 1977
- in OXFORD LITERARY REVIEW 4(2):3-14 1980
- in Politics, Philosophy, Culture* 1988, p110-124
- in Foucault Live* 1989, p137-155 (entitled "The End of the Monarchy of Sex")

55. Interview: Powers and Strategies ("Pouvoirs et strategies", REVOLTES LOGIQUES Volume 4, 1977)
- in Morris, Meaghan and Patton, Paul, eds. Michel Foucault: Power, Truth and Strategy. Sydney: Feral Publications, 1979, p49-58
- in Power/Knowledge* 1980, p134-145

56. Interview: Prison Talk ("Entretiens sur la prison: le livre et sa methode", MAGAZINE LITTERAIRE 101:27-33 1975)
- in RADICAL PHILOSOPHY 16:10-15 1977
- in Power/Knowledge* 1980, p37-54

57. Interview: Questions of Method (Perrot, Michell, ed. L'impossible prison: Recherches sur le systeme penitentiare au XIXe siecle. Paris: Seuil, 1980)
- in IDEOLOGY AND CONSCIOUSNESS 8:3-14 Spring 1981
- in Baynes, Kenneth and others, eds. After Philosophy: End or Transformation? Cambridge: MIT Press, 1987, p100-118
- in Burchall, Graham and others, eds. The Foucault Effect: Studies in Governmentality. London: Harvester Wheatsheaf, 1991, p73-86

58. Interview: Questions on Geography ("Questions a Michel Foucault sur la geographie", HERODOTE Volume 1, 1976)
- in Power/Knowledge* 1980, p63-77

59. Interview: Revolutionary Action: "Until Now" ("Par dela le bien et le mal", ACTUEL 14:42-47 1971)
- in Language, Counter-Memory, Practice* 1977, p218-233

60. Interview: Rituals of Exclusion
- in PARTISAN REVIEW 38(2):192-200 1971 (entitled "A Conversation with Michel Foucault")
- in Foucault Live* 1989, p63-72

61. Interview: Sex, Power and the Politics of Identity
in THE ADVOCATE August 7, 1984, p26

62. Interview: Sexual Choice, Sexual Act: Foucault and Homosexuality
in SALMAGUNDI 58/59:10-24 Fall 1982/Winter 1983
in Politics, Philosophy, Culture* 1988, p286-303
in Foucault Live* 1989, p211-231

63. Interview: Sexual Morality and the Law ("La loi de la pudeur", RECHERCHES 37:69-82 April 1979
in Politics, Philosophy, Culture* 1988, p271-285

64. Interview: Social Security (Securite sociale: l'enjeu. Paris: Syros, 1983)
in Politics, Philosophy, Culture* 1988, p159-177

65. Interview: Sorcery and Madness (LE MONDE April 23, 1976)
in Foucault Live* 1989, p107-111

66. Interview: Space, Knowledge and Power
in SKYLINE March 1982, p16-19
in The Foucault Reader* 1984, p239-256

67. Interview: Structuralism and Post-Structuralism
in TELOS 55:195-211 Spring 1983
in Politics, Philosophy, Culture* 1988, p17-46 (entitled "Critical Theory/Intellectual History")

68. Interview: The Anxiety of Judging (LE MOUVEL OBSERVATEUR May 30, 1977)
in Foucault Live* 1989, p157-178

69. Interview: The Archeology of Knowledge (MAGAZINE LITTERAIRE April/May 1969)
in Foucault Live* 1989, p45-56

70. Interview: The Birth of a World (LE MONDE May 3, 1969)
in Foucault Live* 1989, p57-61

71. Interview: The Concern for the Truth (MAGAZINE LITTERAIRE 207:18-23 May 1984)
in Politics, Philosophy, Culture* 1988, p255-267
in Foucault Live* 1989, p293-308

72. Interview: The Discourse of History (LES LETTRES FRANCAISES June 15, 1967)
in Foucault Live* 1989, p11-33

73. Interview: The Discourse on Power (with Duccio Trombadori)
in Remarks on Marx* 1991, p147-182

74. Interview: The Ethic of Care for the Self as a Practice of Freedom
in PHILOSOPHY AND SOCIAL CRITICISM 12(2/3):112-131 Summer 1987

75. Interview: The Functions of Literature (LE MONDE September 16, 1986)
in Politics, Philosophy, Culture* 1988, p307-313
in Foucault Live* 1989, p113-119 (entitled "On Literature")

76. Interview: The Masked Philosopher (LE MONDE April 6, 1980)
in Politics, Philosophy, Culture* 1988, p323-330
in Foucault Live* 1989, p193-202

77. Interview: The Minimalist Self
in Politics, Philosophy, Culture* 1988, p3-16

78. Interview: The Order of Things (LES LETTRES FRANCAISES March 31, 1966)
in Foucault Live* 1989, p1-10

79. Interview: The Politics of Crime ("Crimes et chatiments en URSS et ailleurs", NOUVEL OBSERVATEUR January 26, 1976, p34-37)
in PARTISAN REVIEW 43:453-459 Fall 1976
in Foucault Live* 1989, p121-130 (entitled "The Politics of Soviet Crime")

80. Interview: The Return of Morality (LES NOUVELLES June 28-July 5, 1984)
in RARITAN 5:8+ Summer 1985
in Politics, Philosophy, Culture* 1988, p242-254
in Foucault Live* 1989, p317-331

81. Interview: The Subject, Knowledge and the "History of Truth" (with Duccio Trombadori)
in Remarks on Marx* 1991, p43-82

82. Interview: Truth and Power (based on the two essays "Verite et pouvoir", ARC 70:16-26 1977 and "La fonction politique de l'intellectuel", POLITIQUE-HEBDO Volume 274, 1976)
in CRITIQUE OF ANTHROPOLOGY 4(13/14):131-138 1977
in Morris, Meaghan and Patton, Paul, eds. Michel Foucault: Power, Truth and Strategy. Sydney: Feral Publications, 1979, p29-48
in Power/Knowledge* 1980, p109-133
in Lemert, Charles, ed. French Sociology. New York: Columbia University Press, 1981, p293-307
in The Foucault Reader* 1984, p51-75

(See also the essay entitled "The Political Function of the Intellectual")

83. Interview: Truth, Power, Self
in Martin, Luther and others, eds. Technologies of the Self. Amherst: University of Massachusetts Press, 1988, p9-15
Related Articles
Hutton, Patrick. "Foucault, Freud and the Technologies of the Self" in Technologies of the Self. Amherst: University of Massachusetts Press, 1988, p121-144

84. Interview: What Calls for Punishment?
in Foucault Live* 1989, p275-292

85. Is It Useless to Revolt?
in PHILOSOPHY AND SOCIAL CRITICISM 8:1-9 Spring 1981

86. Kant on Enlightenment and Revolution

in ECONOMY AND SOCIETY 15(1):88-96 1986

Related Articles

Becker-Cantarino, Barbara. "Foucault on Kant: Deconstructing the Enlightenment?" in Friedrichsmeyer, Sara and Becker-Cantarino, Barbara, eds. The Enlightenment and Its Legacy. Bonn: Bouvier, 1991, p27-33

Gordon, Colin. "Question, Ethos, Event: Foucault on Kant and the Enlightenment", ECONOMY AND SOCIETY 15(1):71-87 1986

Habermas, Jurgen. "Foucault's Lecture on Kant", THESIS ELEVEN 14:4-8 1986

_________. "Taking Aim at the Heart of the Present: On Foucault's Lecture on Kant's 'What is Enlightenment'", UNIVERSITY PUBLISHING 13:5-6 Summer 1984

_________. "Taking Aim at the Heart of the Present: On Foucault's Lecture on Kant's 'What is Enlightenment'" in Habermas, Jurgen. The New Conservatism: Cultural Criticism and the Historians' Debate. Cambridge: MIT Press, 1989, p173-179

87. Language to Infinity ("Le Langage a l'infini", TEL QUEL 15:44-53 1963)

in Language, Counter-Memory, Practice* 1977, p53-68

88. The Life of Infamous Men ("La vie des hommes infames", CAHIERS DU CHEMIN 15 janvier 1977, p12-29)

in Morris, Meaghan and Patton, Paul, eds. Michel Foucault: Power, Truth and Strategy. Sydney: Feral Publications, 1979, p76-91

89. Madness in Childhood

in Jenks, Chris, ed. The Sociology of Childhood: Essential Readings. North Ponfret, VT: Batsford, 1982

90. Means of Correct Training (excerpt from Surveiller et punir*)

in The Foucault Reader* 1984, p188-205

91. Monstrosities in Criticism

in DIACRITICS 1:57-60 Fall 1971

92. My Body, This Paper, This Fire (Response to Jacques Derrida) ("Mon Corps, ce papier, ce feu", PAIDEIA September 1971)

in OXFORD LITERARY REVIEW 4:9-28 1979

Related Articles

Bennington, Geoff. "Cognito Incognito: Foucault's 'My Body, This Paper, This Fire'", OXFORD LITERARY REVIEW 4:5-8 1979

93. Nietzsche, Freud, Marx (in Nietzsche. Paris: Cahiers de Royaumont/Minuit, 1967, p183-197)

in CRITICAL TEXTS 3(2):1-5 Winter 1986

94. Nietzsche, Genealogy, History ("Nietzsche, la genealogie, l'histoire", in Hommage a Jean Hyppolite. Paris: Presses Universitaires de France, 1971, p145-172)
in Language, Counter-Memory, Practice* 1977, p139-164
in SEMIOTEXT(E) 3(1):78-94 1978
in The Foucault Reader* 1984, p76-100
Related Article
Berlin, James. "Revisionary History: The Dialectical Method", PRE/TEXT 8(1/2):47-61 Spring/Summer 1987
Cook, Deborah. "Nietzsche and Foucault on Ursprung and Genealogy", CLIO 19(4):299-309 Summer 1990

95. Of Other Spaces
in DIACRITICS 16(1):22-27 Spring 1986

96. Omnes et singulatim: Toward a Criticism of "Political Reason"
in McMurrin, Sterling, ed. The Tanner Lectures on Human Values, Volume 2. Salt Lake City: University of Utah Press, 1981, p223-254
in Politics, Philosophy, Culture* 1988, p58-85 (entitled "Politics and Reason")

97. On Popular Justice: A Discussion with Maoists ("Sur la justice populaire: debat avec les maos", in Nouveau fascisme, nouvelle democratie. [np] 1972)
in Power/Knowledge* 1980, p1-36

98. On Revolution
in PHILOSOPHY AND SOCIAL CRITICISM 8(1):5-9 Spring 1981

99. On the Archaeology of the Sciences ("Sur l'archeologie des sciences: reponse au cercle d'epistemologie", CAHIERS POUR L'ANALYSE 9:5-44 1968)
in THEORETICAL PRACTICE 3/4:108-127 1971

100. Orders of Discourse (L'ordre du discours: lecon inaugurale au College de France prononcee le 2 decembre 1970. Paris: Gallimard, 1971)
in SOCIAL SCIENCE INFORMATION 10(2):7-30 1971
in Archaeology of Knowledge* 1972 (printed as an appendix) (entitled "The Discourse on Language")
in Young, Robert, ed. Untying the Text: A Post-Structuralist Reader. Boston: Routledge and Kegan Paul, 1981, p51-76 (entitled "The Order of Discourse")
in Adams, Hazard and Searle, Leroy, eds. Critical Theory Since 1965. Tallahassee: University Presses of Florida, 1986, p148-162 (entitled "The Discourse on Language")

101. Other Spaces: The Principles of Heterotopia
in LOTUS INTERNATIONAL 48/49:9-17 1985/86

102. Panopticism (excerpt from Discipline and Punish*)
in The Foucault Reader* 1984, p206-213

103. Photogenic Painting

in CRITICAL TEXTS 6(3):1-12 1989

104. The Political Function of the Intellectual ("Verite et pouvoir" ARC 70:16-26 1977)

in RADICAL PHILOSOPHY 17:12-14 1977

(See also the essay entitled "Truth and Power")

105. The Political Technology of Individuals

in Martin, Luther and others, eds. Technologies of the Self. Amherst: University of Massachusetts Press, 1988, p145-162

Related Articles

Hutton, Patrick. "Foucault, Freud and the Technologies of the Self" in Technologies of the Self. Amherst: University of Massachusetts Press, 1988, p121-144

106. The Politics of Health in the Eighteenth Century ("La politique de la sante au XVIIIe siecle", in Les Machines a querir*. Paris: Institut de l'Environnement, 1976, p11-21)

in Power/Knowledge* 1980, p166-182

in The Foucault Reader* 1984, p273-290

107. Power and Norm: Notes (Notes on a lecture delivered at the College de France, March 28, 1973)

in Morris, Meaghan and Patton, Paul, eds. Michel Foucault: Power, Truth and Strategy. Sydney: Feral Publications, 1979, p59-66

108. Preface

in Herculine Barbin: Being the Recently Discovered Memoirs of a Nineteenth Century French Hermaphrodite. New York: Random House, 1980

109. A Preface to Transgression ("Preface a la transgression", CRITIQUE 195/196:751-769 1963)

in Language, Counter-Memory, Practice* 1977, p29-52

110. The Prose of the World

in DIOGENES 53:17-37 Spring 1966

111. The Repressive Hypothesis (excerpt from Histoire de la sexualite, I*)

in The Foucault Reader* 1984, p301-330

112. Right of Death and Power Over Life (excerpt from Histoire de la sexualite, I)

in The Foucault Reader* 1984, p258-272

113. Sexual Discourse and Power

in Alexander, Jeffrey and Seidman, Steven, eds. Culture and Society: Contemporary Debates. New York: Cambridge University Press, 1990, p199-204

114. Sexuality and Solitude

in LONDON REVIEW OF BOOKS 3(9):3-7 May 21, 1981

in Blonsky, Marshall, ed. On Signs. Baltimore: Johns Hopkins University Press, 1985, p365-372

115. The Subject and Power

<u>in</u> CRITICAL INQUIRY 8(4):787+ Summer 1982

<u>in</u> Dreyfus, Hubert and Rabinow, Paul. <u>Michel Foucault: Beyond Structuralism and Hermeneutics</u>. Chicago: University of Chicago Press, 1983, p208-226

<u>in</u> Wallis, Brian, ed. <u>Art After Modernism: Rethinking Representation</u>. Boston: The New Museum of Contemporary Art, 1984, p416-433

<u>Related Articles</u>

Maslan, Mark. "Foucault and Pragmatism", RARITAN 7(3):94-114 Winter 1988

116. Technologies of the Self

<u>in</u> Martin, Luther and others, eds. <u>Technologies of the Self</u>. Amherst: University of Massachusetts Press, 1988, p16-49

<u>Related Articles</u>

Hutton, Patrick. "Foucault, Freud and the Technologies of the Self" <u>in</u> <u>Technologies of the Self</u>. Amherst: University of Massachusetts Press, 1988, p121-144

Ronell, Avital. "The Worst Neighborhood of the Real: Philosophy-Telephone-Contamination", DIFFERENCES 1(1):125-145 Winter 1989

117. Theatrum Philosophicum ("Theatrum Philosophicum", CRITIQUE 282:885-908 1970)

<u>in</u> <u>Language, Counter-Memory, Practice</u>* 1977, p165-196

118. This is Not a Pipe ("Ceci n'est pas une pipe", CAHIERS DU CHEMIN Volume 2, 1968)

<u>in</u> OCTOBER 1:6-21 1976

119. Two Lectures (January 7, 1976 and January 14, 1976)

<u>in</u> <u>Power/Knowledge</u>* 1980, p78-108

120. War in the Filigree of Peace: Course Summary (unpublished College de France course summary)

<u>in</u> OXFORD LITERARY REVIEW 4(2):15-19 1980

121. We "Other Victorians" (excerpt from <u>Histoire de la sexualite, I</u>*)

<u>in</u> <u>The Foucault Reader</u>* 1984, p292-300

122. The West and the Truth of Sex ("L'occident et la verite du sexue", LE MONDE 5:24 November 1976)

<u>in</u> SUB-STANCE 28:5-9 1978

123. What is an Author? ("Qu'est-ce qu'unauteur?", BULLETIN DE LA SOCIETE FRANCAISE DE PHILOSOPHIE 63:73-104 1969)

<u>in</u> PARTISAN REVIEW 42(4):603-614 1975

<u>in</u> <u>Language, Counter-Memory, Practice</u>* 1977, p113-138

<u>in</u> Harari, Josue, ed. <u>Textual Strategies: Perspectives in Post-Structuralist Criticism</u>. Ithaca, NY: Cornell University Press, 1979, p141-160

<u>in</u> <u>The Foucault Reader</u>* 1984, p101-120

in Adams, Hazard and Searle, Leroy, eds. Critical Theory Since 1965. Tallahassee: University Presses of Florida, 1986, p138-147

in Davis, Robert and Schleifer, Ronald, eds. Contemporary Literary Criticism: Literary and Cultural Studies. New York: Longman, 1989, p262-276

in Mukerji, Chandra and Schudson, Michael, eds. Rethinking Popular Culture: Contemporary Perspectives in Cultural Studies. Berkeley: University of California Press, 1991, p446-464

Related Articles

Lamarque, P. "The Death of the Author: An Analytical Autopsy", BRITISH JOURNAL OF AESTHETICS 30(4):319-331 October 1990

Nehamas, A. "What an Author Is", JOURNAL OF PHILOSOPHY 83(11):685-692 November 1986

_________. "Writer, Text, Work, Author" in Cascardi, Anthony, ed. Literature and the Question of Philosophy: Essays. Baltimore: Johns Hopkins University Press, 1987, p267-291

Pappas, Nicholas. "Authorship and Authority", JOURNAL OF AESTHETICS AND ART CRITICISM 47(4):325-332 Fall 1989

Sheridan, Alan. "The Death of the Author" in Appignanesi, Lisa, ed. Ideas from France: The Legacy of French Theory. London: Free Association Books, 1989, p41-48

Thwaites, Tony. "Words in Collision", AUMLA: JOURNAL OF THE AUSTRALASIAN UNIVERSITIES LANGUAGE AND LITERATURE ASSOCIATION 73:193-204 May 1990

Walker, C. "Feminist Literary Criticism and the Author", CRITICAL INQUIRY 16(3):551-571 Spring 1990

124. What is Enlightenment? (based on an unpublished French manuscript)

in The Foucault Reader* 1984, p32-50

INDEX TO SECTION II.

Introduction

The numbers in the index refer to the entries in Section II which includes essays, interviews and excerpts from the books of Foucault. Keywords from the titles have been used in the index. When there are no words in the title indicating the subject matter, "title enrichment terms" (in the manner used by ART AND HUMANITIES CITATION INDEX) are used to reflect the area covered in the work.

ADORNO 31
AESTHETICS 32, 118 see also ART, FILM, LITERATURE, PAINTING
ANXIETY 68
ARCHAEOLOGY 2, 69, 70, 99
ART 3, 103, 118
ASYLUM 6
ATTICA 49
AUTHOR 123
BARBIN 108
BATAILLE 109
BINSWAGER 15
BIOLOGY 13
BODY 7, 14, 36, 92 see also SEXUALITY
BOULEZ 12
CANUILHEIM 20
CHASTITY 4 see also SEXUALITY
CHILDHOOD 89
CONDEMNED 7 see also PRISON, PUNISHMENT
CONFINEMENT 22, 39 see also PRISON, PUNISHMENT
CRIME 79 see also PRISON, PUNISHMENT
CRITICAL THEORY 67
CRITICISM 48. 91, 96
CULTURE 34
CUVIER 13
DEATH 112
DELINQUENCY 27 see also CONDEMNED, CRIME, PRISON, PUNISHMENT
DEMONSTRATIONS 9
DERRIDA 92 see also POSTSTRUCTURALISM
Discipline and Punish 7, 8, 10, 14, 27, 90, 102
DISCOURSE 24, 72, 73, 100, 113
DREAM 15
ENLIGHTENMENT 86, 124
ETHICS 33, 51, 53, 74 see also MORALITY
EXISTENCE 15, 32

EXPERIENCE 44
FABLE 5
FILM 23, 40
FRANCE 35, 37
FREEDOM 74
FREUD 93
FRIENDSHIP 42
FROMANGER 103
GENEALOGY 51, 94
GEOGRAPHY 58
GOVERNMENT 21 see also POLITICS
HEALTH 106
HEIDEGGER 15
HETEROTOPIA 101
HISTORY 24, 31, 34, 70, 72, 94 see also INTELLECTUAL HISTORY
History of Sexuality 111, 112, 121
HOLDERLIN 19
HOMOSEXUALITY 62 see also SEXUALITY
HORKHEIMER 31
HUMAN NATURE 26
IDENTITY 61
ILLEGALITIES 27 see also CRIME, DELINQUENCY
INDIVIDUALS 105
INFINITY 87
INSTITUTIONS 10
INTELLECTUAL HISTORY 67 see also HISTORY, INTELLECTUALS
INTELLECTUALS 28, 104 see also INTELLECTUAL HISTORY
INTERVIEWS 29 - 84
IRAN 47
JUDGEMENT 68
JUSTICE 26, 97 see also LAW
KANT 86
KNOWLEDGE 2, 25, 48, 66, 69, 70, 81, 119
LANGUAGE 18, 19, 87
LAW 1, 9, 63 see also JUSTICE
LIFESTYLE 42
LITERATURE 18, 19, 75, 123
MADNESS 6, 16, 65, 89, 114 see also PSYCHIATRY
Madness and Civilization 6, 16, 22
MAGRITTE 118
MAOISTS 97
MARCUSE 31
MARX 93

MEMORY 40
METHOD 57
MORALITY 63, 80 see also ETHICS
MUSIC 12
NIETZSCHE 93, 94
ORDER 78, 100
PAINTING 103
PANOPTICISM 102
PEACE 120
PHILOSOPHY 20, 25, 76, 117
PLEASURE 33
POLEMICS 52
POLITICS 24, 35, 52, 53, 61, 79, 96, 104 - 106 see also GOVERNMENT, REVOLUTION
POSTSTRUCTURALISM 67 see also STRUCTURALISM
POWER 17, 26, 28, 35 - 37, 50, 54, 55, 61, 66, 73, 82, 83, 107, 112, 113, 115, 119
PRISON 39, 49, 56 see also CONFINEMENT, PUNISHMENT
PROSE 110 see also WRITING
PSYCHIATRY 1, 39 see also MADNESS
PUNISHMENT 57, 84 see also CONDEMNED, CONFINEMENT, PRISON
REASON 96
REPRESSION 111
REVOLUTION 47, 59, 85, 86, 98 see also POLITICS
RIVIERE 46
SARTRE 41
SCIENCES 99
SELF 74, 77, 83, 116 see also IDENTITY, INDIVIDUALS
SEXUALITY 4, 11, 23, 43, 54, 61 - 63, 111 - 114, 121, 122 see also BODY, HOMOSEXUALITY
SOCIAL SECURITY 64
SOLITUDE 114
SORCERY 65
SPACE 66, 95, 101
STRUCTURALISM 37, 67 see also POSTSTRUCTURALISM
SUBJECT 81, 115
TECHNOLOGY 105, 116
This is not a Pipe 118
THOUGHT 48
TRAINING 90
TRANSGRESSION 109 see also CRIME, DELINQUENCY
TRUTH 3, 45, 71, 81 - 83
WAR 120
WRITING 123 see also PROSE, LITERATURE

BOOKS ABOUT FOUCAULT

Arac, Jonathan, ed. After Foucault: Humanistic Knowledge, Postmodern Challenges. New Brunswick, NJ: Rutgers University Press, 1988

Ball, Stephen, ed. Foucault and Education: Disciplines and Knowledge. New York: Routledge, 1990

Bannet-Tavor, Eve. Structuralism and the Logic of Dissent: Barthes, Derrida, Foucault, Lacan. Urbana: University of Illinois Press, 1989

Baudrillard, Jean. Forget Foucault. New York: Semiotext(e), 1987

Bernauer, James. Michel Foucault's Force of Flight: Toward an Ethics for Thought. Atlantic Highland, NJ: Humanities Press International, 1990

Bernauer, James and Rasmussen, David, eds. The Final Foucault. Cambridge: MIT Press, 1987

Boyne, Roy. Foucault and Derrida: The Other Side of Reason. Boston: Unwin Hyman, 1990

Burchell, Graham and others, eds. The Foucault Effect: Studies in Governmentality. London: Harvester Wheatsheaf, 1991

Carroll, David. Paraesthetics: Foucault, Lyotard, Derrida. New York: Methuen, 1987

Chua Beng Huat. Reading Foucault as a Conservative. Singapore: Department of Sociology, National University of Singapore, 1986

Cooper, Barry. Michel Foucault, an Introduction to the Study of His Thought. New York: Edwin Mellen Press, 1981

Cousins, Mark and Hussain, Athar. Michel Foucault. New York: St. Martin's Press, 1984

Deleuze, Gilles. Foucault. Minneapolis: University of Minnesota Press, 1988

Diamond, Irene and Quinby, Lee, eds. Feminism & Foucault: Reflections on Resistance. Boston: Northeastern University Press, 1988

Dollimore, Jonathan. Sexual Dissidence: Augustine to Wilde, Freud to Foucault. New York: Oxford University Press, 1991

Dreyfus, Hubert and Rabinow, Paul. Michel Foucault, Beyond Structuralism and Hermeneutics. Chicago: University of Chicago Press, 1982

Eribon, Didier. Michel Foucault. Cambridge: Harvard University Press, 1991

Foote, Catherine. Toward a New Understanding of the Problem of Spousal and Child Support After Separation And Divorce Through Michel Foucault's Analytics Of Power. Toronto: Faculty of Social Work, University of Toronto, 1986

Gane, Mike, ed. Towards a Critique of Foucault. New York: Routledge & Kegan Paul, 1986

Grumley, John. History and Totality: Radical Historicism from Hegel to Foucault. New York: Routledge, 1989

Gutting, Gary. Michel Foucault's Archaeology of Scientific Reason. New York: Cambridge University Press, 1989

Hewitt, Michael. Social Policy and the Politics of Life: Foucault's Account of Welfare. Hatfield, England: School of Social Sciences, Hatfield Polytechnic, 1982 28p

Honneth, Axel. The Critique of Power: Reflective Stages in a Critical Social Theory. Cambridge: MIT Press, 1991

Hoy, David, ed. Foucault: A Critical Reader. New York: Basil Blackwell, 1986

Kusch, Martin. Foucault's Strata and Fields: An Investigation into Archaeological and Genealogical Science Studies. Boston: Kluwer Academic, 1991

Lecourt, Dominique. Marxism and Epistemology: Bachelard, Canguilhem and Foucault. London: New Left Books, 1975

Lemert, Charles and Gillan, Garth. Michel Foucault: Social Theory as Transgression. New York: Columbia University Press, 1982

Lentricchia, Frank. Ariel and the Police: Michel Foucault, William James, Wallace Stevens. Madison: University of Wisconsin Press, 1988

Major-Poetzl, Pamela. Michel Foucault's Archaeology of Western Culture: Toward a New Science of History. Chapel Hill: University of North Carolina Press, 1983

Martin, Luther and others, eds. Technologies of the Self: A Seminar with Michel Foucault. Amherst: University of Massachusetts Press, 1988

Megill, Allan. Prophets of Extremity: Nietzsche, Heidegger, Foucault, Derrida. Berkeley: University of California Press, 1985

Merquior, J.G. Foucault. London: Fontana Press, 1991

Michel Foucault, Philosopher: Essays. New York: Harvester Wheatsheaf, 1992

Minson, Jeffrey. Genealogies of Morals: Nietzsche, Foucault, Donzelot and the Eccentricity of Ethics. London: Macmillan, 1985

Morris, Meaghan and Patton, Paul, eds. Michel Foucault: Power, Truth, Strategy. Sydney: Feral Publications, 1979

O'Farrell, Clare. Foucault: Historian or Philosopher? Basingstoke: Macmillan, 1989

O'Hara, Daniel. Radical Parody: American Culture and Critical Agency After Foucault. New York: Columbia University Press, 1992

Poster, Mark. Critical Theory and Poststructuralism: In Search of a Context. Ithaca, NY: Cornell University Press, 1989

__________. Foucault, Marxism and History: Mode of Production Versus Mode of Information. New York: Blackwell, 1984

Quinby, Lee. Freedom, Foucault and the Subject of America. Boston: Northeastern University Press, 1991

Racevskis, Karlis. Michel Foucault and the Subversion of Intellect. Ithaca, NY: Cornell University Press, 1983

Rajchman, John. Michel Foucault: The Freedom of Philosophy. New York: Columbia University Press, 1985

Ray, S. The Modern Soul: Michel Foucault and the Theological Discourse of Gordon Kaufman and David Tracy. Philadelphia: Fortress Press, 1987

Sawicki, Jana. Disciplining Foucault: Feminism, Power and the Body. New York: Routledge, 1991

Scott, Charles. The Question of Ethics: Nietzsche, Foucault, Heidegger. Bloomington: Indiana University Press, 1990

Sheridan, Alan. Michel Foucault: The Will to Truth. New York: Tavistock, 1980

Shumway, David. Michel Foucault. Boston: Twayne, 1989

Smart, Barry. Foucault, Marxism and Critique. Boston: Routledge & Kegan Paul, 1983

__________. Michel Foucault. New York: Tavistock, 1985

Stauth, Georg. Revolution is Spiritless Times: An Essay on the Inquiries of Michel Foucault on the Iranian Revolution. Singapore: Department of Sociology, National University of Singapore, 1991

Stratton, Jon. Writing Sites: A Genealogy of the Postmodern World. London: Harvester Wheatsheaf, 1990

Wuthnow, Robert and others, eds. Cultural Analysis: The Work of Peter L. Berger, Mary Douglas, Michel Foucault and Jurgen Habermas. Boston: Routledge & Kegan Paul, 1984

BIBLIOGRAPHIES

Clark, Michael. Michel Foucault, an Annotated Bibliography: Tool Kit for a New Age. New York: Garland, 1983

Harari, Josue. Structuralists and Structuralism: A Selected Bibliography of French Contemporary Thought, 1960-1970. Ithaca, NY: Diacritics, 1971

Miller, Joan. French Structuralism: A Multidisciplinary Bibliography. New York: Garland, 1981

Nordquist, Joan. Michel Foucault: A Bibliography. Santa Cruz, CA: Reference and Research Services, 1986 60p

ARTICLES ABOUT FOUCAULT

1. **Aladjem, Terry.** "The Philosopher's Prism: Foucault, Feminism and Critique", POLITICAL THEORY 19(2):277-291 May 1991
2. **Alcoff, Linda.** "Feminist Politics and Foucault: The Limits to a Collaboration" in Dallery, Arleen and Scott, Charles, eds. Crises in Continental Philosophy. Albany: State University of New York Press, 1990, p69-86
3. _________. "Justifying Feminist Social Science", HYPATIA 2(3):107+ Fall 1987
4. **Allen, Barry.** "Government in Foucault: The Unsociological Concept of Power in His Works", CANADIAN JOURNAL OF PHILOSOPHY 21(4):421-440 December 1991
5. **Amariglio, J.** "The Body, Economic Discourse and Power: An Economist's Introduction to Foucault", HISTORY OF POLITICAL ECONOMY 20(4):583-613 1988

   Birken, Lawrence. "Foucault, Marginalism and the History of Economic Thought: A Rejoinder to Amariglio", HISTORY OF POLITICAL ECONOMY 22(3):557-569 Fall 1990
6. **Ansell-Pearson, Keith.** "The Significance of Michel Foucault's Reading of Nietzsche: Power, the Subject and Political Theory", NIETZSCHE STUDIEN 20:267-283 1991
7. **Atkinson, T.** "Phantoms of the Studio", ART JOURNAL 13(1):49-62 1990
8. **Babty, Ian.** "Nietzsche, Derrida and Foucault" in Babty, Ian and Yates, Timothy, eds. Archaeology After Structuralism: Post-Structuralism and the Practice of Archaeology. New York: Routledge, 1990
9. **Bacchi, C.** "Feminism and the Eroticization Of the Middle Class", WOMENS STUDIES INTERNATIONAL FORUM 11(1):43+ 1988
10. **Bahr, E.** "In Defense of Enlightenment: Foucault and Habermas", GERMAN STUDIES REVIEW 11(1):97-109 1988
11. **Balbus, Isaac.** "Discipling Women: Michel Foucault and the Power of Feminist Discourse" in Benhabib, Seyla and Cornell, Drucilla, eds. Feminism as Critique: On the Politics of Gender. Minneapolis: University of Minnesota Press, 1987, p110-126
12. **Balides, C.** "Foucault in the Field of Feminism", CAMERA OBSCURA 22:138-149 January 1990
13. **Barrett, M.** "The Concept of 'Difference'", FEMINIST REVIEW 26:29+ Summer 1987
14. **Barrish, Philip.** "Accumulating Variation: Darwin's 'On the Origin of Species' and Contemporary Literary and Cultural Theory", VICTORIAN STUDIES 34(4):431-453 Summer 1991

15. **Bartkowski, Frances.** "Speculations on the Flesh: Foucault and the French Feminists" in Genova, Judith, ed. Power, Gender, Values. Edmonton: Academic, 1987, p69-84

16. **Becker-Cantarino, Barbara.** "Foucault on Kant: Deconstructing the Enlightenment?" in Friedrichsmeyer, Sara and Becker-Cantarino, Barbara, eds. The Enlightenment and Its Legacy. Bonn: Bouvier, 1991, p27-33

17. **Bell, D.** "Michel Foucault: A Philosopher for All Seasons", HISTORY OF EUROPEAN IDEAS 14(3):331-346 May 1992

18. **Bell, Vikki.** "'Beyond the Thorny Question': Feminism, Foucault and the Desexualisation of Rape", INTERNATIONAL JOURNAL OF THE SOCIOLOGY OF LAW 19(1):83-100 February 1991

19. **Bellour, Raymond.** "H.G./F.", GRAND STREET 10(3):79-80 1991

20. **Berlin, James.** "Revisionary History: The Dialectical Method", PRE/TEXT 8(1/2):47-61 Spring/Summer 1987

21. **Bernauer, James.** "Beyond Life and Death: On Foucault's Post-Auschwitz Ethic", PHILOSOPHY TODAY 32:128-142 Summer 1988

22. **________.** "Michel Foucault's Ecstatic Thinking", PHILOSOPHY AND SOCIAL CRITICISM 12(2/3):156-193 Summer 1987

23. **________.** "Oedipus, Freud, Foucault: Fragments of an Archaelogy of Psychoanalysis" in Levin, David, ed. Pathologies of the Modern Self: Postmodern Studies on Narcissism, Schizophrenia and Depression. New York: New York University Press, 1987, p349-362

24. **________.** "The Prisons of Man: An Introduction to Foucault's Negative Theology", INTERNATIONAL PHILOSOPHICAL QUARTERLY 27:365-380 December 1987

25. **Bersani, L.** "Pedagogy and Pederasty" in Poirier, Richard, ed. Raritan Reading. New Brunswick, NJ: Rutgers University Press, 1990, p1-7

26. **Bevis, Phil and others.** "Archaelogizing Genealogy: Michel Foucault and the Economy of Austerity", ECONOMY AND SOCIETY 18(3):323-345 August 1989

27. **Birmingham, Peg.** "Local Theory" in Dallery, Arleen and Scott, Charles, eds. The Question of the Other: Essays in Contemporary Continental Philosophy. Albany: State University of New York Press, 1989, p205-212

28. **Blair, Carole.** "The Statement: Foundation of Foucault's Historical Criticism", WESTERN JOURNAL OF SPEECH COMMUNICATION 51(4):364-383 Fall 1987

29. **Blair, Carole and Cooper, Martha.** "The Humanist Turn in Foucault's Rhetoric of Inquiry", QUARTERLY JOURNAL OF SPEECH 73(2):151-171 May 1987

30. **Bogard, William.** "Discipline and Deterrence: Rethinking Foucault on the Question of Power in Contemporary Society", SOCIAL SCIENCE JOURNAL 28(3):325-346 July 1991

31. **Bordo, Susan.** "Docile Bodies, Rebellious Bodies: Foucauldian Perspectives of Female Psychopathology" in Silverman, Hugh, ed. The Politics of Difference. Albany: State University of New York Press, 1991, p203-217

32. **Botwinick, Aryeh.** "Nietzsche, Foucault and the Prospects of Postmodern Political Philosophy", MANUSCRITO 12(2):117-154 October 1989

33. **Bove, Paul.** "Power and Freedom: Opposition and the Humanities", OCTOBER 53:78-92 Summer 1990

34. **Boyne, R.** "Michel Foucault, Politics, Philosophy", THEORY, CULTURE AND SOCIETY 6(3):471+ August 1989

35. **Bracken, Christopher.** "Coercive Spaces and Spatial Coercions: Althusser and Foucault", PHILOSOPHY AND SOCIAL CRITICSM 17(3):229-241 1991

36. **Bradbury, R.** "What is Post-Structuralism?", INTERNATIONAL SOCIALISM 41:147+ Winter 1988

37. **Braidotti, R.** "Ethics of Sexual Difference: Foucault and Irigaray", AUSTRALIAN FEMINIST STUDIES 3:1+ Summer 1986

38. **Brancaforte, Benito.** "Americo Castro and Michel Foucault's 'Filosofia del sospetto'" in Ricapito, Joseph, ed. Hispanic Studies in Honor of Joseph H. Silverman. Newark, DE: Juan de la Cuesta, 1988, p371-379

39. **Breuer, Stefan.** "Foucault and Beyond: Towards a Theory of the Disciplinary Society", INTERNATIONAL SOCIAL SCIENCE JOURNAL 41(2):235-247 May 1989

40. **Brock, D.** "Sex Debates: Toward Feminist Epistemology", ATLANTIS 13(1):98+ Fall 1987

41. **Buker, Eloise.** "Hidden Desires and Missing Persons: A Feminist Deconstruction of Foucault", WESTERN POLITICAL QUARTERLY 43(4):811-832 December 1990

42. **Burke, F.** "Aesthetics and Postmodern Cinema", CANADIAN JOURNAL OF POLITICAL AND SOCIAL THEORY 12(1):70+ 1988

43. **Burrell, Gibson.** "Modernism, Post Modernism and Organizational Analysis 2: The Contribution of Michel Foucault", ORGANIZATION STUDIES 9(2):221-235 1988

44. **Butler, Judith.** "Foucault and the Paradox of Bodily Inscriptions", JOURNAL OF PHILOSOPHY 86(11):601-607 November 1989

45. ________. "Lana's 'Imitation': Melodramatic Repetition and the Gender Performative", GENDERS 9(1):1-18 Fall 1990

46. ________. "Variations on Sex and Gender: Beauvoir, Wittig and Foucault" in Benhabib, Seyla and Cornell, Drucilla, eds. Feminism as Critique: On the Politics of Gender. Minneapolis: University of Minnesota Press, 1987, p128-142

47. **Callinicos, A.** "Foucault's Third Theoretical Displacement", THEORY, CULTURE AND SOCIETY 3(3):171+ 1986

48. **Cameron, A.** "Redrawing the Map: Early Christian Territory After Foucault", JOURNAL OF ROMAN STUDIES 76:266-271 1986

49. **Casey, Edward.** "The Place of Space in 'The Birth of the Clinic'", JOURNAL OF MEDICINE AND PHILOSOPHY 12:351-356 November 1987

50. **Chessick, Richard.** "Kohut and the Contemporary Continental Tradition: A Comparison of Kohut with Lacan and Foucault" in Buirski, Peter, ed. Frontiers of Dynamic Psychotherapy: Essays in Honor of Arlene and Lewis R. Wolberg. New York: Brunner/Mazel, 1987

51. **Clark, E.** "Foucault, the Fathers and Sex", JOURNAL OF THE AMERICAN ACADEMY OF RELIGION 56(4):619-641 Winter 1988

52. **Clifford, Michael.** "Crossing (Out) the Boundary: Foucault and Derrida on Transgressing", PHILOSOPHY TODAY 31:223-233 Fall 1987

53. **Close, Anthony.** "Centering the De-Centerers: Foucault and Las Meninas", PHILOSOPHY AND LITERATURE 11(1):21-36 April 1987

54. **Cobley, Evelyn.** "Toward History as Discontinuity: The Russian Formalists and Foucault", MOSAIC 20(2):41-56 Spring 1987

55. **Cohen, Ed.** "Foucauldian Necrologies: 'Gay' 'Politics'? Politically Gay?" TEXTUAL PRACTICE 2(1):87-101 Spring 1988

56. **Colburn, Kenneth, jr.** "Desire and Discourse in Foucault: The Sign of the Fig Leaf in Michelangelo's David", HUMAN STUDIES 10(1):61-79 1987

57. **Coles, Romand.** "Foucault's Dialogical Artistic Ethos", THEORY, CULTURE, SOCIETY 8(2):99-120 May 1991

58. **Connell, B.** "Scheherezade's Children: Foucault", ARENA 78:139+ 1987

59. **Constable, M.** "Foucault and Walzer: Sovereignty, Strategy and the State", POLITY 24(2):269-293 Winter 1991

60. **Cook, Deborah.** "History as Fiction: Foucault's Politics of Truth", JOURNAL OF THE BRITISH SOCIETY FOR PHENOMENOLOGY 22(3):139-147 October 1991

61. _________. "The Limits of Histories", CANADIAN JOURNAL OF POLITICAL AND SOCIAL THEORY 11(3):46+ Fall 1987

62. _________. "Madness and the Cogito: Derrida's Critique of 'Folie et Deraison'", JOURNAL OF THE BRITISH SOCIETY FOR PHENOMENOLOGY 21(2):164-174 May 1990

63. _________. "Nietzsche and Foucault on Ursprung and Genealogy", CLIO 19(4):299-309 Summer 1990

64. _________. "Nietzsche, Foucault, Tragedy", PHILOSOPHY AND LITERATURE 13(1):140-150 April 1989

65. _________. "Remapping Modernity", BRITISH JOURNAL OF AESTHETICS 30(1):35-45 January 1990

66. _________. "The Turn Towards Subjectivity: Michel Foucault's Legacy", JOURNAL OF THE BRITISH SOCIETY FOR PHENOMENOLOGY 18:215-225 October 1987

67. _________. "Umbrellas, Laundry Bills and Resistance, the Place of Foucault's Interviews in His 'Corpus'", CLIO 21(2):145-155 Winter 1992

68. **Cook, Jon.** "Fictional Fathers" in Radstone, Susannah, ed. Sweet Dreams: Sexuality, Gender and Popular Fiction. London: Lawrence & Wishart, 1988, p137-164

69. **Cooper, Martha.** "Rhetorical Criticism and Foucault's Philosophy of Discursive Events", CENTRAL STATES SPEECH JOURNAL 39(1):1-16 Spring 1988

70. **Copjec, J.** "The Orthopsychic Subject: Film Theory and the Reception of Lacan", OCTOBER 49:56+ Summer 1989

71. **Corlett, William, jr.** "Pocock, Foucault, Forces of Reassurance", POLITICAL THEORY 17(1):77-90 February 1989

72. **Cresap, Steven.** "Michel Foucault" in McCaffery, Larry, ed. Postmodern Fiction: A Bio-Bibliographical Guide. New York: Greenwood Press, 1986, p360-363

73. **Cressy, D.** "Foucault, Stone, Shakespeare and Social History", ENGLISH LITERARY RENAISSANCE 21(2):121-133 Spring 1991

74. **Culler, Jonathan.** "Political Criticism" in Wood, David, ed. Writing the Future. London: Routledge, 1990, p192-204

75. **Dallmayr, Fred.** "Democracy and Post-Modernism", HUMAN STUDIES 10(1):143-170 1987

76. **Dallmayr, Fred and Hinkle, Gisela.** "Foucault in Memoriam (1926-1984)", HUMAN STUDIES 10(1):3-13 1987

77. **D'Amico, Robert.** "Text and Context: Derrida and Foucault on Descartes" in Fekete, John, ed. The Structural Allegory: Reconstructive Encounters with the New French Thought. Minneapolis: University of Minnesota Press, 1984, p164-182

78. **Davidson, Arnold.** "How to do the History of Psychoanalysis: A Reading of Freud's Three Essays on the Theory of Sexuality", CRITICAL INQUIRY 13(2):252-277 Winter 1987

79. ________. "Sex and the Emergence of Sexuality", CRITICAL INQUIRY 14(1):16-48 Autumn 1987

80. **Davidson, L.** "Psychologism: The Case of Schizophrenia", PRACTICE 6(2):2+ Fall 1988

81. **Davis, C.** "Our Modern Identity: The Formation of the Self", MODERN THEOLOGY 6:159-171 January 1990

82. **Davis, Karen.** "I Love Myself When I am Laughing: A New Paradigm for Sex", JOURNAL OF SOCIAL PHILOSOPHY 21(2/3):5-24 Fall/Winter 1990

83. **Dean, Mitchell.** "Foucault's Obsession with Western Modernity", THESIS ELEVEN 14:44-61 1986

84. **Dews, Peter.** "Foucault and the Frankfurt School" in Appignanesi, Lisa, ed. Ideas from France: The Legacy of French Theory. London: Free Association Books, 1989, p71-80

85. ________. "Foucault and the French Tradition of Historical Epistemology", HISTORY OF EUROPEAN IDEAS 14(3):347-363 May 1992

86. ________. "The Return of the Subject in Late Foucault", RADICAL PHILOSOPHY 51:37-41 Spring 1989

87. **Diawara, Manthia.** "Reading Africa Through Foucault: V.Y. Mudimbe's Reaffirmation of the Subject", QUEST: PHILOSOPHICAL DISCUSSIONS 4(1):74-93 June 1990

88. ________. "Reading Africa Through Foucault: V.Y. Mudimbe's Reaffirmation of the Subject", OCTOBER 55:79-92 Winter 1990

89. **Diprose, R.** "The Use of Pleasure in Constitution of Body", AUSTRALIAN FEMINIST STUDIES 5:94+ Summer 1987

90. **Docherty, T.** "Criticism, History, Foucault", HISTORY OF EUROPEAN IDEAS 14(3):365-378 May 1992

91. **Dollimore, Jonathan.** "The Cultural Politics of Perversion: Augustine, Shakespeare, Freud, Foucault", GENDERS 8:2-16 July 1990

92. **Dreyfus, Hubert.** "Foucault's Critique of Psychiatric Medicine", JOURNAL OF MEDICINE AND PHILOSOPHY 12:311-333 November 1987

93. ________. "On the Ordering of Things: Being and Power in Heidegger and Foucault", SOUTHERN JOURNAL OF PHILOSOPHY 28(9):83-96 1990
Bruzina, R. "Comment" SOUTHERN JOURNAL OF PHILOSOPHY 28(9):97-104 1990

94. ________. "Studies of Human Capacities Can Never Achieve Their Goal" in Margolis, Joseph and others, eds. Rationality, Relativism and the Human Sciences. Dordrech: Nijhoff, 1986, p3-22

95. **Dubois, M.** "The Governance of the Third World", ALTERNATIVES 16(1):1+ Winter 1991

96. **Dumm, Thomas.** "The Politics of Post-Modern Aesthetics: Habermas Contra Foucault", POLITICAL THEORY 16:209-228 May 1988

97. **Earle, W.** "Foucault: The Use of Pleasure as Philosophy", METAPHILOSOPHY 20(2):169-177 April 1989 Ia His Sex 2

98. **Eco, Umberto.** "Language, Power, Force" in Eco, Umberto. Travels in Hyperreality: Essays. New York: Harcourt, Brace, Jovanovich, 1986, p239-255

99. **Edmunds, Lowell.** "Foucault and Theognis", CLASSICAL AND MODERN LITERATURE: A QUARTERLY 8(2):79-91 Winter 1988

100. **Ferry, Luc and Renaut, Alain.** "French Nietzscheanism" in Ferry, Luc and Renaut, Alain. French Philosophy of the Sixties: An Essay on Antihumanism. Amherst: University of Massachusetts Press, 1990, p68-121

101. **Finkelstein, Joanne.** "Biomedicine and Technocratic Power", HASTINGS CENTER REPORT 20(4):13-16 July/August 1990

102. **Flaherty, Peter.** "(Con)textual Contest: Derrida and Foucault on Madness and the Cartesian Subject", PHILOSOPHY OF THE SOCIAL SCIENCE 16(2):157-175 June 1986

103. **Flynn, Bernard.** "Derrida and Foucault: Madness and Writing" in Silverman, Hugh, ed. *Derrida and Deconstruction*. New York: Routledge, 1989, p201-218

104. ________. "Foucault and the Body Politic", MAN AND WORLD 20:65-84 1984

105. **Flynn, Thomas.** "Foucault and the Politics of Postmodernity", NOUS 23(2):187-198 April 1989

106. ________. "Foucault and the Spaces of History", MONIST 74(2):165-186 April 1991

107. ________. "Foucault as Parrhesiast: His Last Course at the College de France", PHILOSOPHY AND SOCIAL CRITICISM 12(2/3):213-228 Summer 1987

108. ________. "Michel Foucault and the Career of the Historical Event" in Dauenhauer, Bernard, ed. *At the Nexus of Philosophy and History*. Athens: University of Georgia Press, 1987, p173-200

109. **Forbes, Ian and Hockaday, Arthur.** "Warfare Without War: Intervention in the International System", ARMS CONTROL 8:52-72 May 1987

110. **Forrester, John.** "Foucault and Psychoanalysis" in Appignanesi, Lisa, ed. *Ideas from France: The Legacy of French Theory*. London: Free Association Books, 1989, p63-70

111. **Foss, Sonja and Gill, Ann.** "Michel Foucault's Theory of Rhetoric as Epistemic", WESTERN JOURNAL OF SPEECH COMMUNICATION 51(4):384-401 1987

112. **Freiwald, Bina.** "Theorist Know Thyself: Foucault, Habermas and the Unity of Knowledge and Interest" in Valdes, Mario, ed. *Toward a Theory of Comparative Literature*. New York: Peter Lang, 1990, p143-154

113. **Freundlieb, Dieter.** "Rationalism Versus Irrationalism? Habermas's Response to Foucault", INQUIRY 31(2):171-192 June 1988

114. **Frow, John.** "Some Versions of Foucault", MEANJIN 47(1):144-156 Autumn 1988; 47(2):353-365 Winter 1988

115. **Gabriel, K.** "Power in the Contemporary Church in the Sociological Theories of Max Weber, Michel Foucault and Hannah Arendt", CONCILIUM 197:29-38 1988

116. **Game, Ann.** "Foucault: The Subject and Power" in Game, Ann. *Undoing the Social: Towards a Deconstructive Sociology*. Milton Keynes: Open University Press, 1991

117. **Gandelman, C.** "Foucault as Art Historian", HEBREW UNIVERSITY STUDIES IN LITERATURE AND THE ARTS 13(2):266-280 1985

118. **Garland, David.** "Frameworks of Inquiry in the Sociology of Punishment", BRITISH JOURNAL OF SOCIOLOGY 41(1):1-15 March 1990

119. **Gillan, Garth.** "Foucault and Nietzsche: Affectivity and the Will to Power" in Silverman, Hugh and Welton, Donn, eds. *Postmodernism and Continental Philosophy*. Albany: State University of New York Press, 1988, p134-142

120. ________. "Foucault's Philosophy", PHILOSOPHY AND SOCIAL CRITICISM 12(2/3):145-155 Summer 1987
121. **Ginsburg, Mark.** "Contradictions in the Role of Professor as Activist", SOCIOLOGICAL FOCUS 20(2):111-122 April 1987
122. **Gold, Steven.** "Foucault's Critique of Functional Marxism", RE-THINKING MARXISM 3(3/4):297-307 Fall/Winter 1990
123. **Goodheart, Eugene.** "Desire and Its Discontents", PARTISAN REVIEW 55(3):387-403 Summer 1988
124. **Gordon, Colin.** "Question, Ethos, Event: Foucault on Kant and the Enlightenment", ECONOMY AND SOCIETY 15(1):71-87 1986
125. **Gould, James.** "Explanatory Grounds: Marx Versus Foucault", DIALOGOS 25(55):133-138 January 1990
126. **Gress, David.** "Michel Foucault", NEW CRITERION 4(8):19-33 April 1986
127. **Gruber, David.** "Foucault and Theory: Genealogical Critiques of the Subject" in Dallery, Arleen and Scott, Charles, eds. The Question of the Other: Essays in Contemporary Continential Philosophy. Albany: State University of New York Press, 1989, p189-196
128. ________. "Foucault's Critique of the Liberal Individual", JOURNAL OF PHILOSOPHY 86(11):615-621 November 1989
129. **Gutting, Gary.** "Michel Foucault and the History of Reason" in McMullin, Ernan, ed. Construction and Constraint: The Shaping of Scientific Rationality. Notre Dame, IN: University of Notre Dame Press, 1988, p153-188
130. **Habermas, Jurgen.** "The Critique of Reason as an Unmaking of the Human Sciences: Michel Foucault" in Habermas, Jurgen. The Philosophical Discourse of Modernity. Cambridge: MIT Press, 1987, p238-265
131. ________. "Foucault's Lecture on Kant", THESIS ELEVEN 14:4-8 1986
132. ________. "Some Questions Concerning the Theory of Power: Foucault Again" in Habermas, Jurgen. The Philosophical Discourse of Modernity. Cambridge: MIT Press, 1987, p266-293
133. ________. "Taking Aim at the Heart of the Present: On Foucault's Lecture on Kant's 'What is Enlightenment'", UNIVERSITY PUBLISHING 13:5-6 Summer 1984
134. ________. "Taking Aim at the Heart of the Present: On Foucault's Lecture on Kant's 'What is Enlightenment'" in Habermas, Jurgen. The New Conservatism: Cultural Criticism and the Historians' Debate. Cambridge: MIT Press, 1989, p173-179
135. **Hadreas, Peter.** "Foucault and Affirmative Action", PRAXIS INTERNATIONAL 11(2):214-226 July 1991
136. **Halperin, David.** "Is There a History of Sexuality?" HISTORY AND THEORY 28(3):257-274 October 1989

137. **Harpham, Geoffrey.** "Foucault and the Ethics of Power" in Merrill, Robert, ed. Ethics/Aesthetics: Post-Modern Positions. Washington, DC: Maisonneuve Press, 1988, p71-81
138. **Harrison, Paul.** "From Bodies to Ethics", THESIS ELEVEN 16:128-140 1987
139. ________. "Power, Culture and Interpretation", PRAXIS INTERNATIONAL 11(3):340+ October 1991
140. **Hartsock, Nancy.** "Foucault on Power: A Theory for Women" in Nicholson, Linda, ed. Feminism/Postmodernism. New York: Routledge, 1990, p157-174
141. ________. "Postmodernism and Political Change: Issues for Feminist Theory", CULTURAL CRITIQUE 14:15-33 Winter 1989/1990
142. ________. "Rethinking Modernism: Minority Vs. Majority Theory", CULTURAL CRITIQUE 7:187+ Fall 1987
143. **Hatlen, Burton.** "Michel Foucault and the Discourse(s) of English", COLLEGE ENGLISH 50(7):786-801 November 1988
144. **Heath, Stephen.** "The Ethics of Sexual Difference", DISCOURSE 12(2):128-153 Spring/Summer 1990
145. **Hendley, Steve.** "Power, Knowledge and Praxis: A Sartrean Approach to a Foucaultian Problem", MAN AND WORLD 21:171-189 March 1988
146. **Hennessy, Rosemary.** "Materialist Feminism and Foucault: The Politics of Appropriation", RE-THINKING MARXISM 3(3/4):252-274 Fall/Winter 1990
147. **Herr, C.** "'The Strange Reward of All That Discipline': Yeats and Foucault" in Orr, Leonard, ed. Yeats and Postmodernism. Syracuse, NY: Syracuse University Press, 1991, p146-166
148. **Hewitt, Martin.** "Bio-Politics and Social Policy: Foucault's Account of Welfare" in Featherstone, Mike and others, eds. The Body: Social Process and Cultural Theory. London: Sage Publications, 1991, p225-255
149. **Heyer, P.** "Foucault, Marxism and History", LABOUR 18:305+ 1986
150. **Hill, R.** "Foucault's Critique of Heidegger", PHILOSOPHY TODAY 34(4):334-341 Winter 1990
151. **Hinkle, Gisela.** "Foucault's Power/Knowledge and American Sociological Theorizing", HUMAN STUDIES 10(1):35-59 1987
152. **Hinson, M.** "Erasing the Frost of Perrault", HARVARD ARCHITECTURE REVIEW 5:84-86 1986
153. **Hirsch, Eli.** "Knowledge, Power, Ethics", MANUSCRITO 12(2):49-63 October 1989
154. **Hodge, Joanna.** "Habermas and Foucault: Contesting Rationality", IRISH PHILOSOPHICAL JOURNAL 7(1/2):60-78 1990
155. **Hohendahl, Peter.** "Habermas' Philosophical Discourse of Modernity", TELOS 69:49-65 Fall 1986
156. **Hollier, D.** "The Word of God: I Am Dead", OCTOBER 44:75-87 Spring 1988

157. **Honneth, Axel.** "Foucault and Adorno: Two Forms of the Critique of Modernity", THESIS ELEVEN 15:48-60 1986
158. **Hooke, Alexander.** "The Order of Others: Is Foucault's Antihumanism Against Human Action?" POLITICAL THEORY 15:38-60 February 1987
159. **Horowitz, Gad.** "The Foucaultian Impasse: No Sex, No Self, No Revolution", POLITICAL THEORY 15:61-80 February 1987
160. **Hoy, David.** "A History of Consciousness: From Kant and Hegel to Derrida and Foucault", HISTORY OF HUMAN SCIENCES 4:1-25 February 1991
161. **Hull, Richard.** "'I Have No Heavenly Father': Foucauldian Epistemes in the Scarlet Letter", AMERICAN TRANSCENDENTAL QUARTERLY 3(4):309-323 December 1989
162. ________. "The Purloined Letter: Poe's Detective Story vs. Panoptic Foucauldian Theory", STYLE 24:201-214 Summer 1990
163. **Hunt, A.** "Foucault's Expulsion of Law: Toward a Retrieval", LAW AND SOCIAL INQUIRY 17(1):1-38 Winter 1992
164. **Hurley, M.** "The Lockdown of Marion Penitentiary", IN THE PUBLIC INTEREST 7:35+ Spring 1987
165. **Hutton, P.** "The Foucault Phenomenon and Contemporary French Historiography", HISTORICAL REFLECTIONS 17(1):77-102 Winter 1991
166. **Huxley, M.** "Massey, Foucault and the Melbourne Metropolitan Planning Scheme", ENVIRONMENT AND PLANNING: A 21(5):659-661 1989
167. **Ijsseling, S.** "Foucault with Heidegger", MAN AND WORLD 19(4):413-424 1986
168. **Ingram, David.** "Foucault and the Frankfurt School: A Discourse on Nietzsche, Power and Knowledge", PRAXIS INTERNATIONAL 6(3):311-327 October 1986
169. **Isenberg, B.** "Habermas on Foucault: Critical Remarks", ACTA SOCIOLOGICA 34(4):299-308 1991
170. **Jacques, T.** "Whence Does the Critic Speak? A Study of Foucault's Genealogy", PHILOSOPHY AND SOCIAL CRITICISM 17(4):325-344 1991
171. **Johnson, J. and Thiele, L.** "Reading Nietzsche and Foucault: A Hermeneutics of Suspicion?" AMERICAN POLITICAL SCIENCE REVIEW 85(2):581-591 June 1991
172. **Johnston, John.** "Discourse as Event: Foucault, Writing and Literature", MODERN LANGUAGE NOTES 105(4):800-818 September 1990
173. **Judovitz, Dalia.** "Derrida and Descartes: Economizing Thought" in Silverman, Hugh, ed. Derrida and Deconstruction. New York: Routledge, 1989, p40-58
174. **Kaplan, L.** "Unhappy Pierre: Foucault, Parricide and Human Responsibility", NORTHWESTERN UNIVERSITY LAW REVIEW 83(1/2):321-359 Fall/Winter 1989
175. **Kateb, George.** "Individualism, Communitarianism and Docility", SOCIAL RESEARCH 56(4):921-942 Winter 1989

176. **Keeley, James.** "Toward a Foucauldian Analysis of International Regimes", INTERNATIONAL ORGANIZATION 44(1):83-105 Winter 1990
177. **Keenan, Tom.** "The 'Paradox' of Knowledge and Power: Reading Foucault on a Bias", POLITICAL THEORY 15:5-37 February 1987
178. **Kendrick, Christopher.** "Milton and Sexuality: A Symptomatic Reading of Comus" in Nyquist, Mary and Ferguson, Margaret, eds. Re-Membering Milton: Essays on the Text and Traditions. New York: Methuen, 1987, p43-73
179. **Kent, C.** "Michel Foucault: Doing History, Or Undoing It", CANADIAN JOURNAL OF HISTORY 21:371-395 December 1986
180. **Krips, Henry.** "Power and Resistance", PHILOSOPHY OF THE SOCIAL SCIENCES 20(2):170-182 June 1990
181. **Kroker, Arthur.** "The Games of Foucault", CANADIAN JOURNAL OF POLITICAL AND SOCIAL THEORY 11(3):1+ Fall 1987
182. ________. "Modern Power in Reverse Image: The Paradigm Shift of Michel Foucault and Talcott Parsons" in Fekete, John, ed. The Structural Allegory: Reconstructive Encounters with the New French Thought. Minneapolis: University of Minnesota Press, 1984, p74-102
183. **Kurzweil, Edith.** "The Fate of Structuralism", THEORY, CULTURE AND SOCIETY 3(3):113+ 1986
184. ________. "Michel Foucault's History of Sexuality as Interpreted by Feminists and Marxists", SOCIAL RESEARCH 53(4):647-663 Winter 1986
185. **Laffey, J.** "The Politics at Modernism's Funeral", CANADIAN JOURNAL OF POLITICAL AND SOCIAL THEORY 11(3):89+ Fall 1987
186. **LaFountain, Marc.** "Foucault and Dr. Ruth", CRITICAL STUDIES IN MASS COMMUNICATION 6(2):123-137 June 1989
187. **Lamarque, P.** "The Death of the Author: An Analytical Autopsy", BRITISH JOURNAL OF AESTHETICS 30(4):319-331 October 1990
188. **Lash, Scott.** "Genealogy and the Body: Foucault/Deleuze/Nietzsche", in Featherstone, Mike and others, eds. The Body: Social Process and Cultural Theory. London: Sage Publications, 1991, p256-280
189. **Latane, David.** "At Play in the Field of Foucault: A Review of Some Recent Texts", CRITICAL TEXTS 6(1):39-58 1989
190. **Lemert, Charles.** "What's Become of Talk? From Hyman to Foucault" in O'Gorman, Hubert, ed. Surveying Social Life: Papers in Honor of Herbert H. Hyman. Middletown, CT: Wesleyan University Press, 1988, p100-116
191. **Levin, David.** "Body Politic: The Embodiment of Praxis in Foucault and Habermas", PRAXIS INTERNATIONAL 9(1/2):112-132 April/July 1989
192. **Levine, David.** "The F-Word: Foucault's History of Sexuality", INTERNATIONAL LABOR AND WORKING-CLASS HISTORY 41:42-48 Spring 1992
193. **Levy, Silvano.** "Foucault on Magritte on Resemblance", MODERN LANGUAGE REVIEW 85(1):50-56 January 1990

194. **Lilly, R.** "Foucault: Making a Difference", MAN AND WORLD 24(3):267-284 July 1991

195. **Long, F.** "The Blondel-Gilson Correspondence Through Foucault's Mirror", PHILOSOPHY TODAY 35:351-361 Winter 1991

196. **Love, N.** "Foucault and Habermas on Discourse and Democracy", POLITY 22(2):269-293 Winter 1989

197. **Luke, Carmen.** "Epistemic Rupture and Typography: 'The Archaeology of Knowledge' and 'The Order of Things' Reconsidered", SOCIOLINGUISTICS 17(2):141-155 1988

198. **Lunn, Forrest.** "Foucault and the Referent", GNOSIS 3(3):73-88 December 1990

199. **Lynch, M.** "The Body: Thin is Beautiful", ARENA 79:128+ 1987

200. **Lyon, D.** "New Technology and the Limits of Luddism", SCIENCE AS CULTURE 7:122+ 1989

201. **MacIntyre, Alasdair.** "Genealogies and Subversions" in MacIntyre, Alasdair. Three Rival Versions of Moral Enquiry: Encyclopaedia, Genealogy and Tradition. Notre Dame, IN: University of Notre Dame Press, 1990, p32-57

202. **Major-Poetzl, Pamela.** "The Disorder of Things", REVUE INTERNATIONALE PHILOSOPHIE 44(173):93-102 May/August 1990

203. **Marshall, James.** "An Anti-Foundationalist Approach to Discipline and Authority", DISCOURSE 7(2):1-20 April 1987

204. ________. "Foucault and Education", AUSTRALIAN JOURNAL OF EDUCATION 33(2):99-113 August 1989

205. ________. "The Incompatibility of Punishment and Moral Education", JOURNAL OF MORAL EDUCATION 18:144-147 May 1989

206. **Maslan, Mark.** "Foucault and Pragmatism", RARITAN 7(3):94-114 Winter 1988

207. **Matless, D.** "An Occasion for Geography: Landscape, Representation and Foucault's Corpus", ENVIRONMENT AND PLANNING: D: SOCIETY AND SPACE 10(1):41-56 February 1992

208. **McCarthy, Thomas.** "The Critique of Impure Reason: Foucault and the Frankfurt School", POLITICAL THEORY 18(3):437-469 August 1990

209. **McHoul, A.** "Foucault, Garfinkel and Sexual Discourse", THEORY, CULTURE AND SOCIETY 5(1):121+ February 1988
Bailey, Stephen. "A Comment on Alec McHoul's Reading of Foucault and Garfinkel on the Sexual", THEORY, CULTURE AND SOCIETY 5(1):111-118 February 1988

210. **McHugh, Patrick.** "Dialectics, Subjectivity and Foucault's Ethos of Modernity", BOUNDARY 2 16(2):91-108 Winter/Spring 1989

211. **McLaren, Peter.** "Ideology, Science and the Politics of Marxian Orthodoxy: A Response to Michael Dale's 'Stalking a Conceptual Chameleon'", EDUCATIONAL THEORY 37:301-326 Summer 1987

212. **McNay, L.** "The Foucauldian Body and Exclusion of Experience", HYPATIA 6(3):125+ Fall 1991

213. **McWhorter, Ladelle.** "Culture or Nature: The Function of the Term Body in the Work of Michel Foucault", JOURNAL OF PHILOSOPHY 86(11):608-614 November 1989

214. ________. "Foucault's Analytics of Power" in Dallery, Arleen and Scott, Charles, eds. Crises in Continental Philosophy. Albany: State University of New York Press, 1990, p119-126

215. ________. "Foucault's Move Beyond the Theoretical" in Dallery, Arleen and Scott, Charles, eds. The Question of the Other: Essays in Contemporary Continential Philosophy. Albany: State University of New York Press, 1989, p197-204

216. **Megill, Allan.** "The Reception of Foucault by Historians", JOURNAL OF THE HISTORY OF IDEAS 48(1):117-141 January/March 1987

217. **Mellencamp, P.** "Images of Language and Indiscreet Dialogue: The Man Who Envied Women", SCREEN 28:87+ Spring 1987

218. **Mellor, Philip.** "The Application of Michel Foucault to Problems in the Study of Religion", THEOLOGY 91:484-493 November 1988

219. **Mermoz, G.** "Rhetoric and Episteme: Writing About 'Art' in the Wake of Post-Structuralism", ART HISTORY 12(4):497-509 December 1989

220. **Merquior, Jose.** "Notes on the American Reception of Foucault", STANFORD FRENCH REVIEW 15(1/2):25-35 1991

221. **Metzger, Mary.** "Feminism and Foucault: Reflections on Resistance", HYPATIA 5(3):118-114 Fall 1990

222. **Meynell, H.** "On Knowledge, Power and Michel Foucault", HEYTHROP JOURNAL 30(4):419-432 October 1989

223. **Miller, James.** "Carnivals of Atrocity: Foucault, Nietzsche, Cruelty", POLITICAL THEORY 18(3):470-491 August 1990

224. ________. "Foucault: The Secrets of a Man", SALMAGUNDI 88/89:311-332 Fall 1990/Winter 1991

225. ________. "Michel Foucault: The Heart Laid Bare", GRAND STREET 10(3):53-64 1991

226. **Miller, Seumas.** "Foucault on Discourse and Power", THEORIA 76:115-125 October 1990

227. **Minogue, Kenneth.** "Can Radicalism Survive Michel Foucault?" CRITICAL REVIEW 3(1):138-154 Winter 1989

228. **Moi, Toril.** "Power, Sex and Subjectivity: Feminist Reflections on Foucault", PARAGRAPH 5:95-102 1985

229. **Mollica, R.** "Upside-Down Psychiatry: A Genealogy of Mental Health Services" in Levin, David, ed. Pathologies of the Modern Self: Postmodern Studies on Narcissism, Schizophrenia and Depression. New York: New York University Press, 1987, p363-384

230. **Moore, Mary.** "Ethical Discourse and Foucault's Conception of Ethics", HUMAN STUDIES 10(1):81-95 1987
231. **Muller, N. and Cloete, A.** "White Hands: Academic Social Scientists", CRITICAL ARTS 4(2):1+ 1986
232. **Muraro, Luisa.** "On Conflicts and Differences Among Women", HYPATIA 2:139-141 Summer 1987
233. **Nealon, Jeffrey.** "Exteriority and Appropriation: Foucault, Derrida and the Discipline of Literary Criticism", CULTURAL CRITIQUE 21:97-119 Spring 1992
234. **Negin, L.** "Postmodernism", ARENA 95:100+ Winter 1991
235. **Nehamas, A.** "What an Author Is", JOURNAL OF PHILOSOPHY 83(11):685-692 November 1986
236. ________. "Writer, Text, Work, Author" in Cascardi, Anthony, ed. Literature and the Question of Philosophy: Essays. Baltimore: Johns Hopkins University Press, 1987, p267-291
237. **Nettleton, S.** "Power and Pain: The Location of Pain and Fear in Dentistry and the Creation of a Dental Subject", SOCIAL SCIENCE AND MEDICINE 29(10):1183-1190 1989
238. **Newton, Judith.** "Historicisms New and Old: Charles Dickens' meets Marxism, Feminism and West Coast Foucault", FEMINIST STUDIES 16(3):449-470 Fall 1990
239. **Nikolinakos, Derek.** "Foucault's Ethical Quandry", TELOS 83:123-140 Spring 1990
240. **Noujain, Elie.** "History as Genealogy: An Exploration of Foucault's Approach to History", PHILOSOPHY 21(supplement):157-174 1987
241. ________. "History as Genealogy: An Exploration of Foucault's Approach to History" in Griffiths, A., ed. Contemporary French Philosophy. Cambridge: Cambridge University Press, 1987, p157-174
242. **O'Brien, P.** "Michel Foucault's History of Culture" in Hunt, Lynn, ed. The New Cultural History. Berkeley: University of California Press, 1989, p25-46
243. **O'Connor, Tony.** "Foucault and the Transgression of Limits" in Silverman, Hugh, ed. Philosophy and Non-Philosophy Since Merleau-Ponty. New York: Routledge, 1988, p136-150
244. **O'Hara, Daniel.** "Michel Foucault and the Fate of Friendship", BOUNDARY 2 18(1):83-103 Spring 1991
245. **Oliver, K.** "Fractal Politics: How to Use the 'Subject'", PRAXIS INTERNATIONAL 11(2):178+ July 1991
246. **Ophir, Adi.** "Michel Foucault and the Semiotics of the Phenomenal", DIALOGUE 27(3):387-415 Fall 1988
247. ________. "The Semiotics of Power: Reading Michel Foucault's 'Discipline and Punish'", MANUSCRITO 12(2):9-34 October 1989

248. Osborne, Thomas. "Medicine and Epistemology: Michel Foucault and the Liberality of Clinical Reason", HISTORY OF THE HUMAN SCIENCES 5:63-93 May 1992

249. Ostrander, Greg. "Foucault's Disappearing Body", CANADIAN JOURNAL OF POLITICAL AND SOCIAL THEORY 11(1):120+ Winter 1987

250. _________. "Foucault's Disappearing Body" in Kroker, Authur and Kroker, Marilouise, eds. Body Invaders: Panic Sex in America. New York: St. Martin's press, 1987, p169-182

251. O'Sullivan, Gerry. "The Library is on Fire: Intertextuality in Borges and Foucault" in Aizenberg, Edna, ed. Borges and His Successors: The Borgesian Impact on Literature and the Arts. Columbia: University of Missouri Press, 1990, p109-121

252. Paden, Roger. "Foucault's Anti-Humanism", HUMAN STUDIES 10(1):123-141 1987

253. Pappas, Nicholas. "Authorship and Authority", JOURNAL OF AESTHETICS AND ART CRITICISM 47(4):325-332 Fall 1989

254. Parsons, S. "Foucault and the Problem of Kant", PRAXIS INTERNATIONAL 8(3):317-328 October 1988

255. Pasquinelli, C. "Power Without the State", TELOS 68:79+ Summer 1986

256. Paternek, Margaret. "Norms and Normalization: Michel Foucault's Overextended Panoptic Machine", HUMAN STUDIES 10(1):97-121 1987

257. Patton, Paul. "Taylor and Foucault on Power and Freedom", POLITICAL STUDIES 37(2):260-276 June 1989
Taylor, C. "Reply", POLITICAL STUDIES 37(2):277-281 June 1989

258. Payer, P. "Foucault on Penance and the Shaping of Sexuality", STUDIES IN RELIGIOUS SCIENCES 14(3):313-320 1985

259. Pecora, Vincent. "Nietzsche, Genealogy, Critical Theory", NEW GERMAN CRITIQUE 53:104-130 Spring/Summer 1991

260. Pennycok, A. "Culture and Knowledge in International Academic Relations", ALTERNATIVES 15(1):53+ Winter 1990

261. Phelan, Shane. "Foucault and Feminism", AMERICAN JOURNAL OF POLITICAL SCIENCE 34(2):421-440 May 1990

262. Philo, C. "Foucault Geography", ENVIRONMENT AND PLANNING: D: SOCIETY AND SPACE 10(2):137-161 April 1992

263. Pilling, John. "A Little Posthumous Prosperity: Raymond Roussel", PN REVIEW 15(1):43-46 1988

264. Polan, Dana. "Powers of Vision, Visions of Power", CAMERA OBSCURA 18:106-119 September 1988

265. Pollis, Carol. "The Apparatus of Sexuality: Reflections on Foucault's Contributions to the Study of Sex in History", JOURNAL OF SEX RESEARCH 23(3):401-408 August 1987

266. **Porter, Ray.** "Is Foucault Useful for Understanding Eighteenth and Nineteenth Century Sexuality?" CONTENTION: DEBATES IN SOCIETY, CULTURE AND SCIENCE 1(1):61-69 Fall 1991

Poster, Mark. "Response", CONTENTION: DEBATES IN SOCIETY, CULTURE AND SCIENCE 1(1):70-81 Fall 1991

267. **Poster, Mark.** "Foucault and Data Bases", DISCOURSE 12(2):110-127 Spring/Summer 1990

268. ________. "Foucault, Poststructrualism and the Mode of Information" in Krieger, Murry, ed. The Aims of Respresentation: Subject/Text/History. New York: Columbia University Press, 1987, p107-130

269. ________. "Foucault, the Present and History", CULTURAL CRITIQUE 8:105-121 Winter 1987/88

270. ________. "Why Not to Read Foucault", CRITICAL REVIEW 3(1):155-160 Winter 1989

Merquior, J. "Comment" CRITICAL REVIEW 4(1/2):286-289 Winter/Spring 1990

271. **Rabinow, Paul.** "Beyond Ethnography: Anthropology as Nominalism", CULTURAL ANTHROPOLOGY 3(4):355-364 November 1988

272. **Racevskis, Karlis.** "The Conative Function of the Other in 'Les Mots et Les Choses'", REVUE INTERNATIONALE DE PHILOSOPHIE 44(173):231-240 1990

273. ________. "Genealogical Critique: Michel Foucault and the Systems of Thought" in Atkins, Douglas and Morrow, Laura, eds. Contemporary Literary Theory. Amherst: University of Massachusetts Press, 1989, p229-245

274. ________. "Michel Foucault, Rameau's Nephew and the Question of Identity", PHILOSOPHY AND SOCIAL CRITICISM 12(2/3):132-144 Summer 1987

275. **Radhakrishnan, R.** "Towards an Effective Intellectual: Foucault or Gramsci?" in Robbins, Bruce, ed. Intellectuals: Politics/Aesthetics/Academics. Minneapolis: University of Minnesota Press, 1990

276. **Rajchman, John.** "Crisis", REPRESENTATIONS 28:90-98 Fall 1989

277. ________. "Foucault the Philosopher: Ethics and Work" in Rajchman, John. Philosophical Events: Essays of the '80s. New York: Columbia University Press, 1991, p57-67

278. ________. "Foucault's Art of Seeing", OCTOBER 44:89-107 1988

279. ________. "Habermas's Complaint", NEW GERMAN CRITIQUE 45:163-191 Fall 1988

Wolin, R. "On Misunderstanding Habermas, A Response to Rajchman", NEW GERMAN CRITIQUE 49:139-145 Winter 1990

Rajchman, John. "Reply", NEW GERMAN CRITIQUE 49:155-161 Winter 1990

280. Rawlinson, Mary. "Foucault's Strategy: Knowledge, Power and the Specificity of Truth", JOURNAL OF MEDICINE AND PHILOSOPHY 12:371-395 November 1987

281. Ray, Larry. "Foucault, Critical Theory and the Decomposition of the Historical Subject", PHILOSOPHY AND SOCIAL CRITICISM 14(1):69-110 1988

282. Redner, Harry. "The Infernal Recurrence of the Same: Nietzsche and Foucault on Knowledge and Power" in Dascal, Marcelo, ed. Knowledge and Politics. Boulder, CO: Westview Press, 1988, p291-315

283. Renov, M. "Topos Noir: The Spacilization and Recuperation of Disorder", AFTERIMAGE 15:12-15 October 1987

284. Resch, R. "Modernism, Postmodernism and Social Theory: A Comparison of Althusser and Foucault", POETICS TODAY 10(3):510-549 Fall 1989

285. Ricci, N. "The Ends of Woman", CANADIAN JOURNAL OF POLITICAL AND SOCIAL THEORY 11(3):11+ Fall 1987

286. ________. "The Ends of Woman", CANADIAN JOURNAL OF POLITICAL AND SOCIAL THEORY 15(1):301+ 1991

287. Richlin, A. "Zeus and Metis, Foucault, Feminism, Classics", HELOS 18(2):160-180 Fall 1991

288. Richters, A. "Modernity-Postmodernity Controversies: Habermas and Foucault", THEORY, CULTURE AND SOCIETY 5(4):611-643 November 1988

289. Rieder, John. "Class and Power: Foucault's Critique of Marxism", HAWAII REVIEW 12(1):143-150 Spring 1988

290. Riley, P. "Michel Foucault, Lust, Women and Sin in Louis-XIV Paris", CHURCH HISTORY 59(1):35-50 March 1990

291. Rodowick, D. "Reading the Figural", CAMERA OBSCURA 24:11-46 September 1990

292. Ronell, Avital. "The Worst Neighborhoods of the Real: Philosophy-Telephone-Contamination", DIFFERENCES 1(1):125-145 Winter 1989

293. Rorty, Richard. "Foucault/Dewey/Nietzsche", RARITAN 9(4):1-8 Spring 1990

294. ________. "Moral Identity and Private Autonomy: The Case of Foucault" in Rorty, Richard. Essays on Heidegger and Others. New York: Cambridge University Press, 1991, p193-198

295. Rose, Nikolas. "Of Madness Itself: 'Histoire de la folie' and the Object of Psychiatric History", HISTORY OF THE HUMAN SCIENCES 3(3):373-380 October 1990

296. Ross, Stephen. "Belonging to a Philosophic Discourse", PHILOSOPHY AND RHETORIC 19:166-177 1986

297. Rothstein, Eric. "A Novel Path to Pentonville", THE EIGHTEENTH CENTURY: THEORY AND INTERPRETATION 31(1):81-90 Spring 1990

298. Rubenstein, Diane. "Food for Thought: Inetonymy in the Late Foucault", PHILOSOPHY AND SOCIAL CRITICISM 12(2/3):194-212 Summer 1987

299. Said, Edward. "Travelling Theory" in Poirier, Richard, ed. Raritan Reading. New Brunswick, NJ: Rutgers University Press, 1990, p305-308

300. Samuel, Raphael. "Reading the Signs", HISTORY WORKSHOP JOURNAL 32:88-109 Autumn 1991

301. Sawicki, Jana. "Foucault and Feminism: Towards a Politics of Difference", HYPATIA 1:23-36 Fall 1986

302. ________. "Heidegger and Foucault: Escaping Technological Nihilism", PHILOSOPHY AND SOCIAL CRITICISM 13(2):155-173 Winter 1987

303. Sax, Benjamin. "Foucault, Nietzsche, History: Two Modes of the Genealogical Method", HISTORY OF EUROPEAN IDEAS 11:769-781 1989

304. ________. "On the Genealogical Method, Nietzsche and Foucault", INTERNATIONAL STUDIES IN PHILOSOPHY 22(2):129-141 1990

305. Saxton, C. "The Collective Voice as Cultural Voice", CINEMA JOURNAL 26:21+ Fall 1986

306. Scalzo, Joseph. "Campanella, Foucault and Madness in Late-Sixteenth Century Italy", THE SIXTEENTH CENTURY JOURNAL 21(3):360-371 Fall 1990

307. Schaub, Uta. "Foucault, Alternative Presses and Alternative Ideology in West Germany: A Report", GERMAN STUDIES REVIEW 12(1):139-153 1989

308. ________. "Foucault's Oriental Subtext", PMLA: PUBLICATIONS OF THE MODERN LANGUAGE ASSOCIATION OF AMERICA 104(3):306-316 May 1989

309. Schneck, Stephen. "Michel Foucault on Power/Discourse, Theory and Practice", HUMAN STUDIES 10(1):15-33 1987

310. Schor, Naomi. "Dreaming Dissymmetry: Barthes, Foucault and Sexual Difference" in Jardine, Alice, and Smith, Paul, eds. Men in Feminism. New York: Methuen, 1987, p98-110

311. Schrift, Alan. "Genealogy and/as Deconstruction: Nietzsche, Derrida and Foucault on Philosophy as Critique" in Silverman, Hugh and Welton, Donn, eds. Postmodernism and Continental Philosophy. Albany: State University of New York Press, 1988, p193-212

312. Schurmann, Reiner. "Foucault, the Frankfurt School and Habermas: On Constituting Oneself an Anarchistic Subject", PRAXIS INTERNATIONAL 6(3):294-310 October 1986

313. Scott, Charles. "Foucault and the Question of Humanism" in Goicoechea, David and others, ed. The Question of Humanism: Challenges and Possibilities. Buffalo, NY: Prometheus, 1991, p205-213

314. ________. "Genealogy and Difference", RESEARCH IN PHENOMENOLOGY 20:55-66 1990

315. ________. "The Power of Medicine, the Power of Ethics", JOURNAL OF MEDICINE AND PHILOSOPHY 12:335-350 November 1987

316. ________. "The Question of Ethics in Foucault's Thought", JOURNAL OF THE BRITISH SOCIETY FOR PHENOMENOLOGY 22(1):33-43 January 1991

317. **Scott, J.** "Deconstructing Equality vs. Difference: Feminism", FEMINIST STUDIES 14(1):33+ Spring 1988

318. **Seerveld, Calvin.** "Footprints in the Snow", PHILOSOPHIA REFORMATA 56(1):1-34 1991

319. **Seidler, Victor.** "Reason, Desire and Male Sexuality" in Caplan, Patricia, ed. The Cultural Construction of Sexuality. London: Tavistock, 1987, p82-112

320. **Seigel, Jerrold.** "Avoiding the Subject: A Foucaultian Itinerary", JOURNAL OF THE HISTORY OF IDEAS 51(2):273-299 April/June 1990

321. **Selman, Mark.** "Dangerous Ideas in Foucault and Wittgenstein", PHILOSOPHY OF EDUCATION: PROCEEDINGS 44:316-325 1988

322. **Shannon, P.** "The Strategy of Working Class Revolution", ARENA 79:158+ 1987

323. **Shapiro, Gary.** "Translating, Repeating, Naming: Foucault, Derrida and 'The Genealogy of Morals'", in Koelb, Clayton, ed. Nietzsche as Postmodernist: Essays Pro and Contra. Albany: State University Press of New York, 1990, p39-56

324. **Sheridan, Alan.** "The Death of the Author" in Appignanesi, Lisa, ed. Ideas from France: The Legacy of French Theory. London: Free Association Books, 1989, p41-48

325. **Silverman, D.** "Making Sense of Ethnomethodology", THEORY, CULTURE AND SOCIETY 6(2):322+ May 1989

326. **Simon, J.** "In Another Know of Wood: Michel Foucault and Sociolegal Studies", LAW AND SOCIAL INQUIRY 17(1):49-55 Winter 1992

327. **Simons, Jon.** "From Resistance to Polaesthetics: Politics after Foucault", PHILOSOPHY AND SOCIAL CRITICISM 17(1):41-56 1991

328. **Singer, Linda.** "True Confessions: Cixous and Foucault on Sexuality and Power" in Allen, Jeffner and Young, Marion, eds. The Thinking Muse: Feminism and Modern French Philosophy. Bloomington: Indiana University Press, 1989, p136-155

329. **Skoll, G.** "Power and Repression", AMERICAN JOURNAL OF SEMIOTICS 8(3):5-29 1991

330. **Smart, Barry.** "On the Subjects of Sexuality, Ethics and Politics in the Work of Foucault", BOUNDARY 2 18(1):201-225 Spring 1991

331. **__________.** "Theory and Analysis after Foucault", THEORY, CULTURE AND SOCIETY 8(2):145-155 May 1991

332. **Snyder, Joel.** "Las Meninas and the Mirror of the Prince", CRITICAL INQUIRY 11(4):539-572 June 1985

333. **Spellmeyer, K.** "Foucault and the Freshman Writer: Considering the Self in Discourse", COLLEGE ENGLISH 51(7):715-729 1989

334. **Spicker, S.** "An Introduction to the Medical Epistemology of Georges Canguilhem: Moving Beyond Michel Foucault", JOURNAL OF MEDICINE AND PHILOSOPHY 12(4):397-411 1987

335. **Stauth, Georg.** "Revolution in Spiritless Times: An Essay on Michel Foucault's Enquiries into the Iranian Revolution", INTERNATIONAL SOCIOLOGY 6(3):259-280 September 1991
336. **Steele, Meili.** "Ontological Turn and Its Ethical Consequences: Habermas and the Poststructuralists", PRAXIS INTERNATIONAL 11(4):428-446 January 1992
337. **Stein, A.** "Literature and Language after the Death of God", HISTORY OF EUROPEAN IDEAS 11:791-795 1989
338. **Steinhart, Eric.** "Self-Recognition and Countermemory", PHILOSOPHY TODAY 33(4):302-317 Winter 1989
339. **Straus, Nina.** "Rethinking Feminist Humanism", PHILOSOPHY AND LITERATURE 14(2):284-303 October 1990
340. **Strong, Beret.** "Foucault, Freud and French Feminism: Theorizing Hysteria as Theorizing the Feminine", LITERATURE AND PSYCHOLOGY 35(4):10-26 1989
341. **Tennessen, Carol.** "Nothing but the Truth: The Case of Pierre Riviere", UNIVERSITY OF TORONTO QUARTERLY 57(2):290-305 Winter 1987/1988
342. **Thiebaux, Marcelle.** "Foucault's Fantasy for Feminists: The Woman Reading" in Mora, Gabriela and Van Hooft, Karen, eds. Theory and Practice of Feminine Literary Theory. Ypsilanti, MI: Bilingual Press, 1982, p44-60
343. **Thiele, Leslie.** "The Agony of Politics: The Nietzschean Roots of Foucault's Thought", AMERICAN POLITICAL SCIENCE REVIEW 84(3):907-925 September 1990
344. ________. "Foucault's Triple Murder and the Modern Development of Power", CANADIAN JOURNAL OF POLITICAL AND SOCIAL THEORY 19:243-260 June 1986
345. **Thwaites, Tony.** "Words in Collision", AUMLA: JOURNAL OF THE AUSTRALASIAN UNIVERSITIES LANGUAGE AND LITERATURE ASSOCIATION 73:193-204 May 1990
346. **Tilley, Christopher.** "Michel Foucault: Towards an Archaeology of Archaeology" in Tilley, Christopher, ed. Reading Material Culture: Structuralism, Hermeneutics and Post-Structuralism. New York: Basil Blackwell, 1990
347. **Tjiattas, Mary and Delaporte, Jean-Pierre.** "Foucault's Nominalism of the Sexual", PHILOSOPHY TODAY 32:118-127 Summer 1988
348. **Turetzky, Philip.** "Immanent Critique", PHILOSOPHY TODAY 33(2):144-158 Summer 1989
349. **Turkel, Gerald.** "Michel Foucault: Law, Power and Knowledge", JOURNAL OF LAW AND SOCIETY 17(2):170-193 1990
350. **Turner, B.** "Foucault and the Crisis of Modernity", THEORY, CULTURE AND SOCIETY 3(3):179+ 1986
351. **Van Den Abbeele, Georges.** "Sade, Foucault and the Scene of Enlightenment Lucidity", STANFORD FRENCH REVIEW 11(1):7-16 Spring 1987

352. **Van Krieken, Robert.** "The Organization of the Soul: Elias and Foucault on Discipline and the Self", ARCHIVES EUROPEENNES DE SOCIOLOGIE 31(2):353-371 1990
353. **Vine, R.** "Foucault's Gay Science", NEW CRITERION 10:64-69 January 1992
354. **Visker, R.** "Can Genealogy be Critical: A Somewhat Unromantic Look at Nietzsche and Foucault", MAN AND WORLD 23(4):441-452 October 1990
355. ________. "From Foucault to Heidegger: A One-Way Ticket", RESEARCH IN PHENOMENOLOGY 21:116-140 1991
356. ________. "Habermas on Heidegger and Foucault: Meaning and Validity in 'The Philosophical Discourse of Modernity'", RADICAL PHILOSOPHY 61:15-32 Summer 1992
357. **Walker, C.** "Feminist Literary Criticism and the Author", CRITICAL INQUIRY 16(3):551-571 Spring 1990
358. **Walkowitz, A.** "Feminist Historiography and the New Historicism", RADICAL HISTORY 43:23-43 January 1989
359. **Wapner, Paul.** "What's Left: Marx, Foucault and Contemporary Problems of Social Change", PRAXIS INTERNATIONAL 9(1/2):88-111 April/July 1989
360. **Weeks, Jeffrey.** "Uses and Abuses of Michel Foucault" in Appignanesi, Lisa, ed. Ideas from France: The Legacy of French Theory. London: Free Association Books, 1989, p49-62
361. **Weightman, John.** "On Not Understanding Michel Foucault", AMERICAN SCHOLAR 58(3):383-406 Summer 1989
362. **Weiss, Harold.** "The Genealogy of Justice and the Justice of Genealogy: Chomsky and Said vs. Foucault and Bove", PHILOSOPHY TODAY 33(1):73-94 Spring 1989
363. **Welch, Sharon.** "A Genealogy of the Logic of Deterrence: Habermas, Foucault and a Feminist Ethic Of Risk", UNION SEMINARY QUARTERLY REVIEW 41(2):13-32 1987
364. **Wellbery, David.** "Theory of Events: Foucault and Literary Criticism", REVUE INTERNATIONALE DE PHILOSOPHIE 41(3/4):420-432 1987 No. 162/163
365. **White, Hayden.** "Foucault's Discourse: The Historiography of Anti-Humanism", LETTRES ROMANES 41(1/2):104-140 1987
366. **White, Ronald.** "Place and Power-Knowledge" in Black, David and others, eds. Commonplaces: Essays on the Nature of Place. Lanham: University Presses of America, 1989, p101-117
367. **White, S.** "Foucault's Challenge to Critical Theory", AMERICAN POLITICAL SCIENCE REVIEW 80(2):419-432 June 1986
368. **Wickham, G.** "Foucault, Power, Left Politics", ARENA 78:146+ 1987
369. ________. "Michel Foucault", THESIS ELEVEN 14:136+ 1986

370. **Woodsworth, Ann.** "Derrida and Foucault: Writing the History of Historicity" in Attridge, Derek and others, eds. Post-Structuralism and the Question of History. Cambridge: Cambridge University Press, 1987, p116-125

371. **Yol Jung, H.** "Question of Moral Subject in Foucault's Theory of Power", CANADIAN JOURNAL OF POLITICAL AND SOCIAL THEORY 11(3):28+ Fall 1987

372. **Yoon, Pyung-Joong.** "Habermas and Foucault: On Ideology/Critique and Power/Knowledge Nexus" KINESIS 17:87-103 Spring 1987

373. **Zerzan, J.** "The Catastrophe of Postmodernism", ANARCHY 30:16+ Fall 1991

BIBLIOGRAPHIES

374. **Bernauer, James.** "Works of Michel Foucault 1954-1984", PHILOSOPHY AND SOCIAL CRITICISM 12(2/3):230-269 Summer 1987

375. **Bernauer, James and Keenan, Thomas.** "The Works of Michel Foucault: 1954-1984" in Bernauer, James and Rasmussen, David, eds. The Final Foucault. Cambridge: MIT Press, 1987, p119-158

376. **Cavallari, H.** "Understanding Foucault: Some Sanity/Other Madness", SEMIOTICA 56(3/4):345-346 1985

377. **Lapointe, Francois.** "Michel Foucault, a Bibliographic Essay", JOURNAL OF THE BRITISH SOCIETY FOR PHENOMENOLOGY 4(2):195-197 1973

378. **Llobena, J.** "Michel Foucault: A Selective Bibliography", CRITIQUE OF ANTHROPOLOGY 4(13/14):139-144 1979

KEYWORD-IN-TITLE INDEX

Introduction

The significant keywords in the titles of the essays in Section IV are listed alphabetically in the index. When there are no words in the title indicating the subject matter, "title enrichment terms" (in the manner used by ART AND HUMANITIES CITATION INDEX) are used to reflect the area covered in the work. Articles of a survey or general nature, those without any specific topic, are listed under "FOUCAULT/GENERAL". The subject search in the index can be narrowed by selecting two or more keywords and comparing the identifying numbers (e.g. FEMINISM and LITERARY THEORY).